MW01006395

A Significant
IMPACT
for Christ

MIKE HILSON

CONTENTS

ACKNOWLEDGMENTS

I want to thank my wife, Tina, who has been my partner in life and in ministry. I love you! To our three boys, Robert, Stephen and Joshua, thank you for taking this journey of ministry with us and having a great attitude about it along the way.

I want to thank Dr. Harry Wood for seeing potential in a young pastor who was lost.

I want to sincerely thank my family at New Life Wesleyan Church for putting up with me as all of these thoughts were developing. Thank you for giving me the freedom to grow as a leader.

Most importantly, I want to thank and praise God!

INTRODUCTION

As a young pastor, a friend asked me a question that I could not answer: "Mike, what is your life goal?" That question took me by surprise. I had viewed myself as a pretty organized, thoughtful and driven person. A leader. However, I instantly realized that this was a pivotal question. My life goal should be the determining factor in every important decision I would ever make, and I didn't even have one.

Now don't get me wrong. I had a number of goals. I was intently working to reach the lost for Christ, to be a good shepherd to the people in my congregation, and to be an excellent leader in my community. I was intently determined to be an excellent husband and father. However, an overarching life goal, I had not considered.

So, I set my mind to work and began to pray about what my life goal should be. I didn't want to name something that was overly centered in my current place of service knowing that I was still in my 20s and all of my circumstances would change. I needed a goal that would be valid for the rest of my life no matter where I lived or what type of job I held. So I spent time in prayer and deep thought about this question. I believe the Holy Spirit gave me an answer:

*"I want to have a significant **IMPACT** for Christ wherever I am serving and whatever I am doing."*

As I began pastoring at New Life Wesleyan Church in La Plata, Maryland, I started to formalize what that phrase meant. While the people I pastored may not have shared my life goal, they needed to know what was driving me to make the choices and decisions I was making. Ultimately, the church took on the same purpose statement I had chosen for my own personal life. At New Life, our goal is to have a significant **IMPACT** for Christ in every community we serve.

From there, sermon series were preached, conversations were had, small group meetings were held, and ultimately, this book was born. This is my attempt to give a clear description of what it means to have an **IMPACT** for Christ, at least from my perspective. If you take these lessons and apply them to your life, you can do more than just survive as a Christian. You can find ways to thrive as a Christian. When these Biblical ideals are followed, there will be a true **IMPACT** on the world around you.

Just imagine, millions of Christians around the world making a significant **IMPACT** with their own lives, in their own ways, using their own unique God-given talents and passions, and in their own communities. The world could not help but be changed. It is an awesome picture of exactly what God wants to do through us.

1

INVITATION

Becoming a part of the family of believers

REACHING GOD

"For God so loved the world that he gave his one and only Son, that whoever believes in him shall not perish but have eternal life. For God did not send his Son into the world to condemn the world, but to save the world through him." (John 3:16-17)

Adam and Eve did not realize how good they had it! They were created by God and placed in a perfect world. God had created a place that perfectly suited His greatest creation. He had created a real paradise in which they could live and rule. Life was truly good.

But that wonderful place was marred by sin. By choosing to disobey God, Adam and Eve caused a separation between them and God. This separation broke the heart of God more than Adam and Eve would ever understand. What was once a beautiful, intimate relationship had become strained and difficult. Adam and Eve were cast out of the Garden of Eden and sent to scratch out a living in the tough soil of a sinful existence.

And so it is that we are born into sin. As descendants of Adam and Eve, we struggle each day with the unintended separation from God that is the result of their sin. It leaves us longing for something that we cannot always describe. Every person, no matter what they might claim, has experienced the yearning in their hearts after something that is beyond them. Throughout the ages, mankind has tried to explain or fill this yearning with anything and everything we can find, yet nothing but God will do the trick. It is a God-shaped vacuum that exists in our hearts, and only God can fill it.

The good news is that God yearns for us as well. In fact, He was so intent on restoring that lost relationship that He provided a new way to establish it. We find in the Bible, in the Gospel of John:

> *For God so loved the world that he gave his one and only Son, that whoever believes in him shall not perish but have eternal life. For God did not send his Son into the world to condemn the world, but to save the world through him. (John 3:16-17)*

Take a minute to absorb that truth. God loves us so much that He was willing to send His own Son to pay the price of our sins. His Son, Jesus, was willing to give His life so that we all might once again experience an intimate relationship. Jesus died for us.

Christianity is, by definition, a religion, but at its core it is not about the structure and ritual of religion. It is all about the relationship. God wants a relationship with you so badly that He paid the ultimate price to make that possible. He is not coming to you, like so many people do, with condemning words or a condescending attitude. He is coming with the gift of forgiveness firmly in hand and freely offered to you. The question now is what will you do with it?

Will you accept God's love for you and establish a relationship with Him?

Or

Will you reject God and leave behind the only chance you will ever have at eternal life?

The choice is yours. I hope you have already decided that a relationship with God is worthwhile. If you have not, please take a look at this 4-step prayer that will help you understand what God is looking for from you.

The Plan of Salvation

"In reply Jesus declared, 'I tell you the truth, no one can see the kingdom of God unless he is born again.'" (John 3:3)

How to be saved:

Confess – Admit that you have sinned.

"For all have sinned and fall short of the glory of God." (Romans 3:23)

Believe – Jesus can and will forgive your sins.

"For the wages of sin is death, but the gift of God is eternal life in Christ Jesus our Lord." (Romans 6:23)

Repent – Change your ways to His ways.

"Repent, then, and turn to God, so that your sins may be wiped out, that times of refreshing may come from the Lord." (Acts 3:19)

Receive – Accept His love for you.

"That if you confess with your mouth, 'Jesus is Lord,' and believe in your heart that God raised Him from the dead, you will be saved." (Romans 10:9)

If you would like to establish a relationship with God today or would like to renew your commitment to your relationship with Him, take a moment and pray this prayer. While there is no magical prayer, this will give you a guide as to what to say as you come before God asking for forgiveness. The issue is your own heart. If you truly want to know Jesus as your Savior, He will hear that in spite of your words. Pray this prayer as a way to call out from your heart to His and make a connection with the Creator:

Lord Jesus, I confess that I have sin in my life. I know I have messed up. Please forgive me. Wash my life clean and allow me to have a relationship with You. Teach me how to live differently and become more like you. Thank you for loving me and thank you for forgiving me. Amen.

If you just prayed that prayer, then let me be the first to say **WELCOME HOME!**

Personal Thoughts:

REACHING FORGIVENESS

"If you confess with your mouth 'Jesus is Lord', and believe in your heart that God raised Him from the dead, you will be saved." (Romans 10:9)

Sometimes the hardest part of building a relationship with God is accepting His forgiveness. Many of us have lived so far away from God and have acted so badly in our lives that we simply cannot believe God will just forgive our sins. We struggle with forgiving ourselves, and that makes believing that God can forgive us even more difficult. This lack of trust in God's willingness to forgive leaves us without the peace and security that should be ours in God's complete forgiveness. We end up living with guilt that we cannot let go, even though it is guilt that God no longer holds against us. In short, we miss the divine peace of God's complete forgiveness.

One thing we should understand right here and now is that we are not alone in this sin problem. There are only two kinds of people in the world: **sinners** and **sinners saved by grace**. If you have found the saving grace of God through Jesus in your life but are concerned about the sin in your past, then please remember that we all have sin in our past. We are alike in that respect. We fall into one of two categories: **sinners** (those who have not found God's forgiveness) and **sinners saved by grace** (those who have found and accepted God's forgiveness).

In order to overcome this inability to accept forgiveness, we need to understand a few things about God.

God Forgives and Forgets

"I, even I, am he who blots out your transgressions, for my own sake, and remembers your sins no more." (Isaiah 43:25)

God's forgiveness is not like ours. We often agree to forgive people for hurting us but we almost never forget. In fact, we often work hard at remembering in detail the entire event so that if we are in a moment when it will be helpful to bring up, we will clearly be able to recall someone else's failure. God simply forgives and forgets.

You see, after God forgives you, He chooses to forget what you have done. If you approach God and ask, "Father, remember that thing I did a few weeks ago in which you forgave me?" His answer will be, "No child, I don't remember that at all." Now let me tell you, that is comforting. There is no need to continue to apologize for the same sin over and over. If God forgives you, it is gone. Disappeared. Absent. History. Over. Done. FORGOTTEN!

God let it go, so why don't you?

God Saves and Separates

"For as high as the heavens are above the earth, so great is his love for those who fear him; as far as the east is from the west, so far has he removed our transgressions from us." (Psalm 103:11-12)

When God saves us, He removes us from our sin. Now, we can crawl back into the mud and the garbage of our former life if we choose, but God does not leave us there. He has made us a new creation. He has removed us from a place of filth and failure. He has lifted us to a level that is acceptable to Him. He can look at us and not see the sin that got us in trouble in the first place. In fact, as far as God is concerned, you are not even the same person. You are someone else altogether, and God sees the new you. He doesn't see your old, sinful self.

God let it go, so why don't you?

God Forgives and Frees

"Therefore, there is now no condemnation for those who are in Christ Jesus, because through Christ Jesus the law of the Spirit of life set me free from the law of sin and death." (Romans 8:1)

When God forgives me of my sin, He frees me from the condemnation that I deserve and sets *"me free from the law of sin and death."* You see, ultimately, only God has the right to judge me. He decides whether I deserve to be condemned or set free. He is the only one in the universe with that authority. If I ask Him to forgive me, He chooses not to condemn me.

Now, it's time for a reality check. While it is true that God will take away the guilt and condemnation your sins deserve, He will often not remove the physical consequences of those sins. Your sin may take a toll on you that is not removed by God's forgiveness.

We all know that smoking greatly increases the likelihood of cancer. If you know this activity can kill you but you choose to smoke anyway, then that is the risk you take. Years later, you may admit that you were wrong to smoke and you may decide to quit, but that doesn't reverse the damage you have already done to your lungs. You may find yourself delivered from the habit and yet forced to accept the consequences of your actions.

God loves you and wants the best for you. However, the fact still remains that our actions have consequences that we already have accepted. God will free you from sin and guilt. God will take away the ultimate condemnation of separation from Him. God will promise you peace on earth and eternity in Heaven. God may not remove the consequences of your sinful actions.

While the consequences may be sobering, the deliverance is nothing less than remarkable. I can be *"free from the law of sin and death."* I can find peace with my Creator, which in turn can help me find peace with myself and others. In God, there is *"no condemnation for those who are in Christ Jesus,"* and that's great news!

God let it go, so why don't you?

Personal Thoughts:

REACHING COMPASSION

"Praise be to the God and Father of our Lord Jesus Christ, the Father of compassion and the God of all comfort, who comforts us in all our troubles, so that we can comfort those in any trouble with the comfort we ourselves have received from God." (2 Corinthians 1:3-4)

Compassion is rightly understood as the act of caring for the needs of others. We see Jesus throughout His ministry expressing a deep compassion for the people around Him. His compassion for them drove Him to heal their sick, raise their dead, teach them how to live, and lead them toward the Father. In fact, it was His compassion for us that brought Him to the earth in the first place. When He was confronted with our lost and sinful state, He set Himself as the source of our salvation. His compassion for you and for me drove Him to the cross, and ultimately, to His death.

His compassion also brought life. From the moment that Jesus came out of that tomb and overcame death, we have been able to access the freedom and fulfillment of eternal life in Christ. His compassion for our lost state not only drove

Him to die so that our sins would be washed clean, but also to rise from the dead so that our existence here and our eternal existence in Heaven would have meaning and purpose. In His death, Jesus paid the price for our sins. In His life, He gives us the hope for victory. If we are to be like Christ, we must become compassionate people. We must understand the mercy and grace that offered us a forgiveness that we did not deserve and work at pointing others toward that same hope. Just as we have found Christ and His forgiveness, we must lead others to Him so that they, too, might be forgiven.

So how do we find compassion in our lives? To be honest, some of us have very little natural compassion for others. We are always hard on ourselves and expect much, so we look at others and think: "why can't they just get their act together?!" But Christ didn't show that type of difficult spirit. He instead showed a compassion that reached out to many who were the last and least in society. We must work at finding compassion in our lives as well. God wired us to be compassionate, but we must work at reaching our potential.

The Source of Compassion

"Praise be to the God and Father of our Lord Jesus Christ, the Father of compassion and the God of all comfort"

As we read this verse, we immediately see that the source of compassion is God Himself. We look to Him for a heart that is filled with compassion for others instead of pursuing comfort for ourselves. Our natural tendency would not be compassion. In fact, our natural tendency would be self-centeredness. Left alone, most of us would tend to look out for "number one" and leave others behind. While human nature seems to run against the tide of compassion, God's nature is centered on it. In His compassion for us, He has done so much that we take for granted. Our health, our loved ones, our jobs, our homes, our freedoms, our salvation, our families, and our friends are all examples of gifts that come from the compassionate heart of God. Even beyond that, there is the strength that comes during times of great trial and stress, the peace in great heartache, and the joy in the midst of great sorrow that also are gifts of our Heavenly Father's compassionate heart. He is our source of compassion and we should be in the habit of asking Him to make us compassionate people.

The Story of Compassion

"who comforts us in all our troubles"

As we look around, we notice that the most compassionate people are often the ones who have endured the most. Simply put, when we go through great difficulty in our lives, we understand the reality of the pain and suffering others experience when they go through something similar. The real story of compassion is the story of our own personal pain. God allows difficulty in our lives and comforts us in the midst of it. He strengthens us to endure and empowers us to find victory. Then He expects us to be understanding when we come across others who are facing a similar crisis. He allows the difficulties in our lives to produce in us a compassion that is willing to reach out and help others.

The Sharing of Compassion

"so that we can comfort those in any trouble with the comfort we ourselves have received from God."

Now for the final question. You know you have faced hard times in your life and you have learned from those difficult experiences. You also know there are others who are facing situations similar to your own. Are you willing to dredge up the painful memories of those hard-learned lessons in order to help others? For some, the initial answer is an absolute NO! For others, there would be an enthusiastic YES! But what about you? God did not allow those difficult experiences in your life just to make you tough. He did it to make you tender. He allowed it to make you understanding. He shaped you to be compassionate, but like so many other things in life, the choice is yours. To use those lessons to show a heart of compassion for others is to bring beauty from an ugly time in our lives. To hide away in the continuing pain of our scars is to allow the hard, calloused hands of bitterness to take a firm grip on the living and loving that is left to be done. Compassion can set you and those you help on the path toward healing and recovery.

"Therefore, as God's chosen people, holy and dearly loved, clothe yourselves with compassion, kindness, humility, gentleness and patience." (Colossians 3:1)

Personal Thoughts:

REACHING FRIENDS AND FAMILY
PART 1

"Pastor, I don't know how to talk to my friends and family about Jesus. I just don't think I can do it." This sentiment is not uncommon. It is truly difficult to share our faith with those closest to us. They know our faults and our past sins. They know we are not perfect, even after we are forgiven. They just know us too well. But we must reach them with the Gospel.

There are so many reasons to work first and hardest in this area.

> **Influence** – Our friends and family are our area of greatest influence. While it is true that they are keenly aware of our faults and flaws, it is also true that they know our hearts and have learned through the years to see when we are sincere about our beliefs. If we can reach anyone, we can reach them.

> **Forgiveness and Peace** – It should stand to reason that if we want anyone to know the peace of being forgiven, it would be our friends and family. Honestly, the argument

that we don't want to offend them pales in comparison to the joy they would find in Christ if we would just get past our fear and tell them about His Grace. Just as we found peace when we knew Christ had forgiven us, they can find peace as well. In the end, they will see and understand the love that motivated us to share Christ even when they did not want to hear.

Eternity – Perhaps the strongest reason for making certain that we share our faith with those who are closest to us is the issue of eternity. Everyone will spend eternity somewhere. If you know Christ as your Savior, you will spend eternity in Heaven with Him. What about our loved ones? Where will they spend eternity? Isn't that a question you would like to be able to answer? Eternity is no small matter and it should be taken seriously. A little discomfort here is in no comparison to an eternity in Heaven.

"OK Pastor, how am I supposed to explain my faith to someone who is so close to me?" This is a fair question. In order to answer it, let's consider three different situations we find in Scripture.

A Traveling Faith

"Those who had been scattered preached the word wherever they went." (Acts 8:4)

"Take the Name of Jesus with You" is the title of an old hymn that we used to sing in church. The idea is simple. Talk about Jesus wherever you go. This is how the faith has traveled for centuries. However, don't get the wrong mental picture of the scripture you see here. It would be a mistake for us to visualize the believers arriving in some unknown town only to immediately begin standing on street corners preaching about Jesus to total strangers. That is just not how a faith that is under persecution from almost every corner of the world grows.

Today, we call it friendship evangelism. As believers moved into new communities, they began to naturally make friends with people around them. They joined the PTO at school, the Country Club, the YMCA or any number of other local organizations. Once there, they met people and formed relationships. AFTER winning their friendship, they shared their faith. I think this is a profound principle.

Evangelism has often been limited to a few outdated methods, such as an event involving some powerful preacher and a series of meetings focused on reaching the lost. This is just not effective today, nor is the old American concept of door-to-door marketing. (I know some of you might be offended and want me to call it door-to door-evangelism, but let's be honest about what is going on here.) Some would even revert back to the old southern favorite, street preaching. (For those who are not familiar with this, it involves a guy in a tie holding a large Bible screaming at the top of his lungs about hellfire and damnation. If it sounds a little offensive to you, then you see the problem.) Truly effective evangelism does not involve any of these. It is a simple matter of friends telling friends about Christ.

This does take a measure of courage. The first objection is usually, "I don't know what to say!" Well, keep in mind that these first century Christians did not have a script that had been prepared for them ahead of time. They did not have memory verses, tracts or even the New Testament. All they had was an experience with the living Christ and a deep desire to talk about Him. It was the personal testimony of that relationship that won over their friends. And so it is today. I know of very few people who found faith in Christ after a long debate over theological principles. However, I know many who have found faith after watching the life of a friend change for the better in the presence of the Master.

You can do this. And by the way, the Holy Spirit will help.

Personal Thoughts:

REACHING FRIENDS AND FAMILY
PART 2

A Bringing Faith

"The following day he arrived in Caesarea. Cornelius was expecting them and had called together his relatives and close friends." (Acts 10:24)

In his powerful book, "Experiencing God," Henry Blackaby makes the point that we should stop asking God to bless what we are doing and start doing what God is blessing. In other words, we should look for the powerful presence of God and go there. The same principle works when trying to reach our friends and family. When the Holy Spirit is present, it is not possible for people to remain neutral on issues of faith. One must either accept the presence of God or reject Him altogether.

In this scripture, we see Cornelius, a Roman centurion, calling on the Apostle Peter for a better understanding of the ministry and forgiveness of Jesus. Cornelius has been in prayer and God has told him to send for Peter. Likewise, Peter has been in prayer and God has told him to go and preach the Good News to Cornelius. Once Cornelius recognized that the presence of God's Spirit was with Peter who was coming to his home, he *"called together his relatives and close friends"* so that they could experience the presence of God with him. Once Peter arrived and spoke, no one was disappointed.

We must understand that Cornelius could have met with Peter alone and received the Holy Spirit. He could have then gone and attempted to explain his experience to his friends and win them over to the Truth of the Gospel. This is the pattern that we often choose. The problem with this approach is that all we are giving to our friends and family is a story or explanation of what we have experienced. When we take them with us, we allow them to share in the experience itself. The simple truth is that there is no substitute for a personal encounter with the Holy Spirit of God. Therefore, we should take our family and friends to any place where we believe the powerful presence of God can be experienced. This could be at a church service, a small group session, a Bible study, a Christian concert, an evangelistic crusade, or even a social event with other Christian friends. Wherever they can experience the God we have accepted is the very place they need to be.

Now, don't miss a simple yet profound truth here. The activity or location is not the issue. The powerful presence of God is the issue. We also can pray that God would move in us whenever we are in the presence of our family and friends. Again, His presence is the issue. In His presence, everything else will fade away. In His presence, only He is lifted up. In His presence, there is power to be new and hope to be different. In His presence, is where we want to live our lives and take our loved ones.

A Living Faith

"I have been reminded of your sincere faith, which first lived in your grandmother Lois and in your mother Eunice and, I am persuaded, now lives in you also." (2 Timothy 1:5)

I really can relate to Timothy here. God has blessed my life with so many wonderful family members who have lived out their faith in front of me. Both of my grandfathers were pastors and wonderful Christians. Both displayed wonderful examples of Christian living and leadership. They were very different people in personality and leadership, but they were both wonderful examples. In today's world, we are truly lacking in good, positive examples of godly living.

This issue of leading people to faith by living a strong faith in front of them is a life-long endeavor. Accomplishing this is not a matter of days, weeks or months. This is a matter of years and decades. It will take years of faithful, consistent living in order to finally see our efforts begin to pay dividends. Timothy's grandmother, Lois, had obviously passed her faith on to her daughter, Eunice, who then had passed it on to her son Timothy. Notice that we are talking about the third generation before broad-based results are achieved. Let me repeat myself, this is a life-long process.

"So why would I worry about this long process when it may take three generations in order for it to be achieved?" While this question seems valid, especially to those of us who lack patience, it is actually the wrong question. You see, with some people it will take a lifetime of living out what we say we believe to convince others that we are truly serious about Christ. These people want to see your faith lived out in real, concrete ways and want to see it lived out for great lengths of time. After years of watching you truly strive in your faith, then they will consider faith in your God. They may even consider making Him their God.

Now, there is a great risk inherent in this lifestyle of evangelism. Decades of righteous living can be nullified by moments of sinful surrender. Satan, the enemy of our souls, will constantly strive to ruin our life-long testimony by throwing in our path the momentary pleasures that tempt us the most. He is no slouch in his effort to lead us astray and make us ineffective witnesses. He is not stupid and he does not give up. In order to live out a lifestyle of faith, we must remain diligent and self-controlled. Even when we find ourselves tired of being good, we must press on so that all those around us will find us faithful to the end. This approach is not easy, nor is it fun, but it is effective.

A Three-Part Plan

Keep in mind that reaching those who are closest to us almost will never be a matter of choosing one of three methods for each person we would like to reach. It is more often a matter of using all three. We must take our faith with us wherever we go **(A Traveling Faith)**, bring our friends and family to the powerful presence of God **(A Bringing Faith)**, and live lives that are worth following **(A Living Faith)**. All of this will be required for a powerful testimony to those who know us best. It is hard. It is painful. It is often a slow process. In the end, we will find that not only have we become a better witness, we have become a better person. Then we may find that those who know us best are most likely to trust our faith and find our Father.

Personal Thoughts:

REACHING COMMUNITIES

"As he approached Jerusalem and saw the city, he wept over it." (Luke 19:41)

One night, many years ago, I found myself sitting alone in a hotel room in Cincinnati, Ohio. I sat with my Bible and looked out the window at the light of the city that night and noticed a bridge. This particular bridge was a double-decker bridge and so there were headlights headed in both directions in a steady stream. Now, you have to remember that I am from a very small town. This was an unusual experience for me. At the time, I was living in a city with a population of about 8,500. This was a big place and that was a lot of cars. While watching those cars cross the bridge, it dawned on me that each set of headlights represented at least one person and likely two. I realized that I was looking at literally thousands of people crossing that bridge. It was then that I sensed God speaking to my spirit: "How many of them know me? How many of them would die before they come to know me? What are you going to do about it?" Needless to say, it was a profound moment.

Since that moment, I have never again seen my ministry as a matter of pastoring a single church. I simply do not believe that God has called us to be part of a single church. I believe that God has called us to reach a community of people. Jesus looks over Jerusalem and weeps. He did not weep for a single church or even for the godly people in the city. He wept over the city and all its people. Jesus saw more than a single group of people. He saw everyone. As we look around us, we are quite often trapped in a habit of seeing only our own group. We see our church, our neighborhood, and our friends. Instead, I think God would challenge us to see more. I think God would challenge us to look down over Jerusalem and see the entire city. I think God would have us see a community that is bursting at the seams with people who need to find His hope and forgiveness.

As I walk through crowds, I often take the time to mentally do an inventory of those around me. If you consider that at best 15-20% of people in the United States of America attend church on any given Sunday, then you have the basis for this exercise. (These statistics are different depending on where you live.) Simply start counting to ten. **One, two**. Alright, now that lists the people who know Jesus as Savior and have experienced the life-altering presence of the Holy Spirit. Now finish counting. **Three, four, five, six, seven**. As you count, look at the faces of the people you count. It is difficult to take someone for granted after looking into their eyes. Consider the families that are involved. Consider the friends and relatives who would be touched and changed for the better if only they knew of God's love for them. **Eight, nine, ten**. Then consider that the last 8 you counted are likely walking without the hope of Christ, without the hope of victory over sin, and without the hope of eternity with God.

When this reality hits home, the change is profound. We stop seeing masses of people, and we start seeing individuals who God loved enough to send His only Son to die. Once we see life in this perspective, we can see the city and weep. Once we understand the significance of our faith in the lives of those around us, we can find the courage to share our faith with them. And when that happens, we truly begin to see that God is the only source of hope in a sin-sick world.

Personal Thoughts:

REACHING INDIVIDUALS

On one occasion an expert in the law stood up to test Jesus. "Teacher," he asked, "what must I do to inherit eternal life?" "What is written in the Law?" [Jesus] replied. "How do you read it?" He answered: "'Love the Lord your God with all your heart and with all your soul and with all your strength and with all your mind'; and, 'Love your neighbor as yourself.'" "You have answered correctly," Jesus replied. "Do this and you will live." But he wanted to justify himself, so he asked Jesus, "And who is my neighbor?" In reply Jesus said: "A man was going down from Jerusalem to Jericho, when he fell into the hands of robbers. They stripped him of his clothes, beat him and went away, leaving him half dead. A priest happened to be going down the same road, and when he saw the man, he passed by on the other side. So too, a Levite, when he came to the place and saw him, passed by on the other side. But a Samaritan, as he traveled, came where the man was; and when he saw him, he took pity on him. He went to him and bandaged his wounds, pouring on oil and wine. Then he put the man on his own donkey, took him to an inn and took care of him. The next day he took out two silver coins and gave them to the innkeeper. 'Look after him,' he said, 'and when I return, I will reimburse you for any extra expense you may have.'" (Luke 10:25-35)

What attracts people to Jesus? Well-meaning Christians have tried many different ways to attract people to the Good News of Jesus Christ, from massive evangelistic crusades to small groups of believers going door-to-door in local neighborhoods. Some of these things are more effective than others and some are less effective. Some things work better in one city or location while others work better in another. It seems like the options in front of us are many and complex. But it really isn't that complicated. Simply put, YOU will attract people to Jesus.

People are attracted or driven away from Jesus by the image of Him they see in us. We are literally walking billboards for Jesus' love. When people look at our lives and see the real love that is only found in the presence of the Holy Spirit, they find themselves intrigued and will listen as we explain His love to them. However, when they look at our lives and see nothing different from the world around them, they are turned off and they tune out.

Jesus understood this concept well. Once when challenged on how to inherit eternal life, Jesus found himself answering the question: *"And who is my neighbor?"* Basically the question could be rephrased to ask, "Who do I have to be nice to?"

or "Who do I have to love?" Jesus answered with a story that we all know very well. In this account of the Good Samaritan, Jesus makes it clear that loving your neighbor is not a matter of saying the right words. Instead, it is a matter of showing the right love. You see, words are simple and often shallow and hollow. Actions speak much louder than words. When we show someone love, we display to them the very nature of Christ Jesus.

Years ago, there was a "Christian" television program called PTL. The hosts of the program were Jim and Tammy Faye Bakker. At the end of each program, they would end with a plastic smile and the words, "God loves you and we do too!" I must tell you that I was never quite convinced that they were sincere. Their words did not ring true. On the other hand, there was my Youth Pastor at First Wesleyan Church. He took me to lunch, talked me through problems, taught me about stage management and sound systems, traveled with me, and basically just invested in my life. When he said, "God loves you and so do I," I believed him. His actions made the words ring true.

Likewise, we must understand that sincerity is more important than intelligence when it comes to winning someone's confidence. As we work to reach people with the Good News of Jesus, we must first convince them that we are real. We must let them see our true hearts, and let them find there a real love for them and a real concern for their future. In winning their trust, we earn the right to share our heart. In sharing our heart, we open the door to offer new life in Christ. In offering new life in Christ, we open the possibility of an eternal hope and an eternal home brought to us through the sacrifice on the cross of Calvary. Jesus has paid the price. The Holy Spirit has tugged at their hearts. All we need to do is show the way.

Personal Thoughts:

2

MATURITY

Growing in maturity to become more like Christ

BECOMING A PRAYER

"This, then, is how you should pray: 'Our Father in heaven, hallowed be your name, your kingdom come, your will be done on earth as it is in heaven. Give us today our daily bread. Forgive us our debts, as we also have forgiven our debtors. And lead us not into temptation, but deliver us from the evil one.'" (Matthew 6:9-13)

"Pastor, please don't ask me to pray. I don't know how." I have heard that request many times through the years. It seems that few forms of speech make people more nervous than being called on to pray. Somehow it seems that in order to pray, we need to have a way with words or the ability to sound "spiritual" as we talk to God. Since many of us don't know how to do that, we find praying a very frightening thought. "What if I say something wrong and make God mad?" or "What if I somehow say something insulting? He is the Ruler of the universe you know!" So we avoid prayer because it just seems too difficult and risky.

Simply put, this fear is born out of a wrong view of prayer. Prayer should never be intimidating. It should be invigorating. Prayer need not be professional. It should be personal. Prayer is our opportunity to stand before the most powerful and loving Being in the universe and speak our minds. We can vent our frustrations to Him, make our requests to Him, give our praises to Him, and just be with Him in a silent moment. All of that is prayer. Prayer is a great thing.

"OK Pastor, fine, prayer is great! But how do I do it? What do I say?" In the long term, we should just speak to God straight from our hearts, but to get started, Jesus gives us a sample prayer we can use.

"Our Father in heaven, hallowed be your name"

We should always start our prayers with praise. God is more than worthy of all the praise we could possibly give Him. He has created us and He has kept us. He is the one who has placed the earth in this wonderfully delicate balance in the universe. He is the one who created this world with such vivid colors and beautiful sights. He is the one who has given us the ability to love and be loved. He also is the one who has provided forgiveness for our sins. He has more than earned our praise. Just as Jesus showed us, each prayer should begin with praise.

"your kingdom come, your will be done on earth as it is in heaven."

Once we have come to Him in prayer and offered our praise to the God of the universe, we need to remember just how great He really is. We should remember how unworthy we are to have a relationship with Him. We can know Him only because He loved us enough to make that relationship possible. He is in charge here and we must submit ourselves to His divine will.

Admittedly, God's will is not always our first choice. His ways are not often our ways and His ideas are not often our ideas. Yet His ways and His ideas are right and best. So our next step in prayer should be to willingly submit to His will and His way. God will always be in control. For our own sake, we need to acknowledge His right to reign in our lives.

"Give us today our daily bread."

There is nothing wrong with asking for God's help. As we pray to Him about the issues of our lives, He hears and helps us through the power and presence of the Holy Spirit. The problem is when we ask selfishly or without submission to His will.

Jesus' example shows us to specifically and practically ask. It is not that we shouldn't ask or expect the miraculous. It is a matter of asking God to fulfill our needs and not our wants. God desires to provide for us everything we need for our daily lives here on earth. He does not want to see us in need of anything. He certainly has the resources to fill our every need. Ask Him and trust Him.

In every circumstance, we must submit to His will. It is no mistake that submission precedes requesting. We, again, must understand that He will provide in accordance with His will. We may not understand or like the provision that God gives us, but we must trust that the Heart of our loving Father has our best interest in mind.

"Forgive us our debts, as we also have forgiven our debtors."

In God's opinion, forgiveness is huge! His act of forgiveness for us cost Him the most precious gift He could give, His son Jesus. Now He calls us to forgive as well. This call is not optional or debatable. God absolutely expects us to forgive others just like He forgave us. Forgiveness is required.

We all know that forgiving someone who has hurt us is difficult. I do not wish to in any way diminish the difficulty of that task. However, we need to compare the cost of our forgiveness to the cost of God's forgiveness. He gave His only Son on a cross so that we could be forgiven. He paid the ultimate price for our forgiveness and now we are called to pay a price of our own. The price will be difficult and steep. The process will be painful and perhaps long. In the end, it makes us more like Him. Forgiveness is required, but like so many other commands from God, it is also healing.

"And lead us not into temptation, but deliver us from the evil one."

In our day-to-day lives, Satan will tempt us to do and say things that are destructive to us as individuals and to our witness as Christians. We find our strength to fight these temptations limited and often insufficient. We struggle but we do not overcome. We strive but we often fail. We work hard at being good and yet we still are bad. Temptation can leave us feeling discouraged and defeated.

God is not the one who tempts us. God understands the temptations we face. He knows the enemy we battle. He knows its cause and its destructive goal. God is aware of our struggle and He will give us a delivering strength if we ask. This strength will carry us through the difficult temptations of our daily lives and will deliver us from the grasp of a temptation that we otherwise would fall into. Our hope and our freedom from the temptations that would so easily entangle us are found in the power and presence of the Holy Spirit in our lives. Every prayer we pray should include a plea to God for more of His delivering presence so that we can face the increasing attacks from the enemy who wants to do us in.

There is a basic structure for prayer, but don't be held captive to this or any other format. Instead, try to use all of the elements Jesus has given us here. In the end, the issue is not how we pray, when we pray, where we pray, or in what position we pray. The issue is that we pray.

Personal Thoughts:

(Take a moment and write out a prayer to God.)

BECOMING A STUDENT

"Do your best to present yourself to God as one approved, a workman who does not need to be ashamed and who correctly handles the word of truth." (2 Timothy 2:15)

Let me give you this verse as it is written in the King James Version of the Bible: *"Study to shew thyself approved unto God, a workman that needeth not to be ashamed, rightly dividing the word of truth" (2 Timothy 2:15 KJV).* Reading these two versions of the same verse gives a clear understanding that God wants us to know and understand His Word. We are called to *"study"* the scriptures so that we are not *"ashamed"* and so that we *"correctly"* handle God's Word.

"So Pastor, how am I supposed to understand the Bible?" I would like to suggest a four-step process of Bible study.

Consume

In order to know the Bible, you must make a regular habit of reading the Bible. King David writes in Psalms:

How can a young man keep his way pure? By living according to your word. I seek you with all my heart; do not let me stray from your commands. I have hidden your word in my heart that I might not sin against you. (Psalm 119:9-11)

Reading God's Word is one way that we know God's will.

Each of us needs to set aside a particular time in our day we will spend reading God's Word. This time should be a quiet time in your house and a time that is not likely to be interrupted or overlooked. For many people, quiet, uninterrupted time comes easiest in the mornings. Therefore, they choose to get out of bed a few minutes early and spend that time reading the Bible. Others find that this time can be carved out just before bedtime each night. No matter when this time comes for you, discipline yourself to keep it. It is a daily appointment with God. Remember that each time you open the Bible and read, you are receiving a message from the very heart of God.

Contemplate

As you set aside time to read the Bible, leave some time to consider what you have read. Again,

King David writes:

> *Oh, how I love your law! I meditate on it all day long.*
> *Your commands make me wiser than my enemies, for*
> *they are ever with me. I have more insight than all my*
> *teachers, for I meditate on your statutes. I have more*
> *understanding than the elders, for I obey your precepts.*
> *(Psalm 119:97-100)*

Notice that King David spends a great deal of time in meditation over the law of God. In the same way, we need to spend time seriously considering what God's Word means for our lives. God can speak to us through His Word, but only if we take the time to consider what He is saying and sit quietly so that we might hear that still, small voice that speaks truth.

Compare

After consuming and contemplating the Word of God, you will find a deeper level of understanding. You will begin to see things that you never noticed or knew before about God and His love and concern for you. You will begin to understand like never before the wisdom of His law and His commandments. In short, the Word of God will begin changing your mind.

Even so, there will be some verses and sections of the Bible that are difficult to understand. You may even spend some time thinking that you understand and yet not certain that you have it right. At this point, I would recommend that you find some Bible study tools that can help you.

The best tools for this are Bible commentaries. A Bible commentary is a printed book of someone's understanding of the meaning of the Bible. A commentary will take a verse-by-verse look at the Bible and will spend many paragraphs or pages explaining the meaning and background of a particular verse. While some are very difficult to read, others are easier to follow. Commentaries are available at all Christian bookstores and online outlets.

Remember, commentaries are only the opinion of a well-educated person. You are looking for absolute truth from God, not a particular author. The commentary will allow you to compare your understanding to the understanding of someone else and perhaps find better understanding in the process.

Comprehend

Whatever you do, don't give up on understanding God's Word. He wants you to comprehend His Word. He wants you to know His will. The Holy Spirit will help you, but at times He will allow you to search for a while so that you spend some time really considering the truth you are learning.

So, consume God's Word. Contemplate God's Word. Compare your thoughts on God's Word. In the end, pray, ask, discuss and study so that you will comprehend the loving and true Word of God in your life.

Personal Thoughts:

BECOMING A THINKER

"The proverbs of Solomon son of David, king of Israel: for attaining wisdom and discipline; for understanding words of insight; for acquiring a disciplined and prudent life, doing what is right and just and fair; for giving prudence to the simple, knowledge and discretion to the young – let the wise listen and add to their learning, and let the discerning get guidance – for understanding proverbs and parables, the sayings and riddles of the wise. The fear of the LORD is the beginning of knowledge, but fools despise wisdom and discipline." (Proverbs 1:1-7)

One of the most common misconceptions about Christians made by non-Christians is that we are not intelligent people. "Surely if they would just think through what they say they believe then they would stop believing." While this concept of the believer may be popular among non-believers, it is simply not true.

God never calls us to turn off our brains and simply follow His messenger in lock-step. Quite the contrary, God commands us through the Apostle Paul to *"not believe every spirit, but test the spirits to see whether they are from God, because many false prophets have gone out into the world" (1 John 4:1).* God calls us to turn our brains on and consider carefully what we know about Him and His Word. God calls us to be thinkers.

Becoming a Christian thinker will require some quiet time. We must take time to really concentrate and think through the issues that we face on a daily basis. Decisions that we make every day have spiritual applications in our lives. The world around us is complex and confusing at times and it is important that we think through what we believe and what that means in our lives.

Tune Out

In order to help us through this, let me begin by suggesting that you take some time to tune out the rest of the world and just contemplate the issues in your life. Honestly, we are constantly surrounded by the noise and clamor of our hurried existence. The radio, the television, the computer, the internet, the kids, the house, the dog, the church, and the community all clamor for a piece of our limited schedule. It can seem almost impossible to find time to stop and think.

Let me encourage you to make time. It will not come by some fluke of scheduling, and if free time does appear that way we are quite capable of filling it with other things. We must make time to consider how God's truth should impact our decisions and lives.

While there may be hundreds of ways to scratch out a little time in your day, I would make a simple suggestion here. When driving home in the car, turn off the radio and spend some time in quiet thought about a major issue in your life. Consider how you would like to react to that issue. Consider how the Bible would encourage you to react to that issue. Ask the famous question: "What Would Jesus Do?" Just take time in the car to think.

Get alone. Get quiet. And Think!

Tune In

As you take this time to think through your life, work with more than just your opinions. While your opinions are there for a reason and they are valid, they are still only your opinions. Take the time to seek out wisdom from others, and most importantly, wisdom from God. Tune in to what God would teach you about a particular issue of focus. Take the time to listen to the thoughts of other Christians on the matter. Do the work of finding well-educated thinkers who have written books on the issue and see what they have to say. Simply put, put work in to your thoughts.

Once you have done this, take the time to tune in to God's Word on the issue. Consider what the Bible might say about what you are facing. Remember, our source of authority on how to live in this world is the Bible. Read it, consider it, think on it. You may find that your decisions change. God's Word and the Holy Spirit may change your mind about some things as you take the time to think through them. At the very least, your decision will be made with more confidence. You will not only know what to do, you will be able to explain why. You will not only know what is right, you will be able to explain why. You will not only know whom you follow, you will know why.

Personal Thoughts:

(List 2-3 issues that you need to take time to think about.)

BECOMING A FOCUSER

As we just mentioned, there are many things that compete for your time and attention. Most of these things are not bad and many are wonderful and worthy endeavors. We are left with too few hours in the day to focus on them all. So how do we decide where to direct our focus? How do we decide which movies or TV channels to watch, music to listen, websites to surf, or magazines to read? The Bible gives us some guidance for these choices in Philippians 4:8. Our focus should be on things that are worthwhile in God's perspective. Things that are true, noble, right, pure, lovely, admirable, excellent, and praiseworthy. These things deserve our attention and focus.

Now, while there is no shortage of programs and images for us to focus on, many of them simply do not pass the Philippians 4:8 test. Many of them are not building us up; instead, they are tearing us down. Many of the things the world would throw at us as simple entertainment, is actually destructive, spiritual weaponry. Satan knows how to turn our minds away from God. He understands that if we remain focused on godly things, we will most likely remain focused on God.

He also understands that if we remain focused on God and godly things, we will do great damage to his kingdom. So his goal is to distract us from the godly and attract us with the sensual.

The process here is really quite simple. Whatever you come in contact with or whatever decision you have to make in your life, you need to ask a series of eight questions:

1. Is this True?

Agreeing with the facts: not false; real or genuine.

The burden of truth should be met by anything we agree to think, say or do. We should be committed to those things that are based in real truth. In fact, if something is not true, it is a waste of our time, reputation and integrity.

2. Is this Noble?

Having, showing, or coming from personal qualities that people admire (such as honesty, generosity, courage, etc.).

Nobility is a lost understanding. We should strive to be noble in all that we do. We should strive to always act in a manner of high moral character. We should be noble in all of our decisions and actions.

3. Is this Right?

Morally or socially correct or acceptable; agreeing with the facts or truth: accurate or correct; speaking, acting, or judging in a way that agrees with the facts or truth.

It almost seems too old-fashioned to think about, but we should always strive to do the right thing. This often means that we don't do the thing that is most profitable, most comfortable, or most popular. It is important that we do what is right.

4. Is this Pure?

Not mixed with anything else; clean and not harmful in any way.

Purity is not considered possible by many in our culture. There seems to be an expectation of impurity instead. It is often assumed that everyone is doing something wrong and so purity must not be that important. On the contrary, the Bible calls us to purity. We should be constantly working to purify our hearts, our motives, and our habits.

5. Is this Lovely?

Attractive or beautiful especially in a graceful way; very good or likable; very pleasing.

Some may say: "Alright, this just sounds too sticky sweet!" Perhaps so, but God calls us to focus on things that are lovely. Focus on things that will inspire love and affection in our lives and the lives of others. Focus on things that will appeal to more than what meets the eye. In other words, our beauty must be real and more than just skin deep.

6. Is this Admirable?

Deserving the highest esteem.

So consider this question: "Do you deserve admiration from the people around you?" Understand the question. It is not a matter of your position; it is a matter of your person. Do you, as a person, deserve admiration? The answer is most likely a mixed bag. In some areas, yes, and in some areas, no. Our goal as Christians is to see the admirable in our lives become the normal and not the exception.

7. Is this Excellent?

Very good: extremely good.

As Christians, we should constantly be striving for the highest quality in our work and ways. We should be who the world looks to as we strive to be the very best version of ourselves. It is the Christian who should be known as a person of highest excellence.

8. Is this Praiseworthy?

Deserving praise: worthy of praise.

This is the "legacy" question. What will people who follow behind you have to say about what you have chosen and what you have done? Will your actions add value to their lives or frustration? Will your choices make their choices better or worse? In other words, will they praise you for a job well done and choices well made or curse you for causing them trouble through your poor choices and actions?

Regardless of the activity or goal, these questions can be applied in every area of our lives and doing so will make a world of difference!

Personal Thoughts:

(List 2-3 issues that may not pass the Philippians 4:8 test.)

BECOMING A DOER

"Do not merely listen to the word, and so deceive yourselves. Do what it says." (James 1:22)

This new morning broke like every other. The army of Israel was standing on one hill while the army of the Philistines was standing on the other. Then the Israelites saw him strut out onto the battle field for what seemed like the hundredth time. Just like he had done for days before, Goliath began to shout his taunting challenges to Saul's army. Like every other day, no one responded. But today something was different. Into the crowd of trembling soldiers had entered a young shepherd. His name was David, and he knew what every other person on that hillside knew; he knew that someone had to deal with that giant. Goliath was no smaller an issue in David's mind than in the minds of others. Death at his hand was no less frightening. The difference is David was willing to act on what others were not.

How many times have we seen that? A situation arises and the solution is obvious but difficult. Everyone wonders who will step up to solve the problem, yet no one comes forward.

While there are few who are willing to do the right thing, there are many who will talk about what needs to be done and wonder out loud why no one will do it. Simply put, there are two kinds of people when it comes to dealing with difficult problems in life. There are those who are "talkers" and those who are "doers."

The Bible speaks often of the need for people who will do the right things in life, even when they are difficult. Time after time, we see heroic characters emerge and deal with the difficult while others simply sit and cower. David vs. Goliath, Moses vs. Pharaoh, Elijah vs. the prophets of Baal are only a few of the great examples of leadership and courage remembered in scripture. God is looking for those who will act on what we know is right.

All too often we fail to act on what we know. We look at the obvious and find it difficult so we avoid doing anything about it. We then begin to wonder why God doesn't change or improve our situation. We ignore the difficult truth that it was our own failure. God, on the other hand, is just waiting for us to get busy at the work He has made so obvious to us. His blessing is on the other side of our sacrifice. His strength is on the other side of our courage and faith.

James tells us, *"Do not merely listen to the word, and so deceive yourselves. Do what it says."* In a blunt command, he reminds us that we are called to do what God says is right. We are called to more than simple belief or understanding. We are called to action. If our habits are not in line with His holiness, we are called to do something about it. If our thoughts are not in line with His purity, we are called to do something about it. If our world is not displaying His love, we are called to do something about it. If our friends are not hearing His Good News, we are called to do something about it.

Well then, what can you do? While the answers to that question can be numerous, keep in mind that we can all do something. In our church, there are cars that need to be parked and babies who need to be rocked. There are children who need to be taught and teenagers who need to be loved. There are shut-ins who need to be visited, poor people who need to be fed, hurting people who need to be helped, lonely people who need to be hugged, and even lost people who need to be found. There is plenty to do. We just have to start doing something about it.

So, today, when we are reminded or confronted with situations that scream for someone to do the right thing, RESPOND! In the words of those great thinkers at Nike, **Just Do It!**

Personal Thoughts:

(List one thing you need to do today.)

BECOMING A TEACHER

"Then Jesus came to them and said, 'All authority in heaven and on earth has been given to me. Therefore go and make disciples of all nations, baptizing them in the name of the Father and of the Son and of the Holy Spirit, and teaching them to obey everything I have commanded you. And surely I am with you always, to the very end of the age.'" (Matthew 28:18-20)

God has called us to teach more often than to preach. We sometimes read this scripture, which is known as the Great Commission, and see in it only a call to convert people to our way of thinking about God. "If we can just get them to pray the sinner's prayer and go to our church, then we will have done our job." Or so the thought goes. In truth, that assessment misses the point of this Great Commission, or great call, on our lives.

It is true that we are called to tell others about Jesus and to encourage them to consider His claims about God and God's love for us. It is also true that we hope to bring those around us into a relationship with God that would include regular times of corporate worship in a church. However, let's not miss the true calling here. Jesus calls us to *"make disciples of all nations"* and to teach *"them to obey"* everything He has taught us. A great deal of evangelism is a matter of good teaching.

Make Disciples

A disciple is more than just a believer. A disciple is a committed follower. A believer is someone who can recognize the reality of the existence of God. Just like someone can recognize that you really exist and therefore believe in you, people can simply recognize the existence of God and believe in Him. This is not a matter of committed following; it is simple, factual believing.

On the other hand, some believe in God and His word to the point that they are willing to change their lives to match His will. This is the central point of discipleship. Disciples realize that what they believe about God must impact the way they act in the world. This belief must, in fact, impact every part of who they are and what they do. A disciple is constantly considering ways to become more compliant, more connected, and more comparable to the God in whom his belief, and trust, is placed. A disciple is more than just a believer. We are called to lead people to discipleship, not just belief.

Teaching them to Obey

Obedience is not a popular word in our English vocabulary. We are trained throughout our lives to be self-supporting and individualistic. Obedience can just feel wrong. Many would argue against obedience saying something like, "I want to make my own decisions and make up my own mind!" However, God has called us to learn and teach obedience, popular or not.

Now teaching someone to obey God's law is not as easy as it would seem. While God demands and expects obedience, He does not force obedience. It is still our choice. Sin is always a possibility. So we are confronted with a difficult situation. We need to teach people to willingly choose obedience to God's laws and ways. We must somehow impress on others the benefits of obedient living.

At this point, we could give up. Classes will often fail. Lectures rarely work. Arguments make the situation worse. So how do we teach? Let me give you a simple phrase to remember as you strive to teach others to follow Christ.

More is Caught than is Taught

This simple phrase can help us avoid one of the biggest hindrances to effective teaching. You see, we often will try and teach people to act in ways that we are not willing to act ourselves. We will try and teach them to accept things that we ourselves have not accepted. This is entirely ineffective. The old phrase, "Do as I say not as I do," has never been an effective teaching tool. People will tend to do what you do, and not really hear what you say.

With this in mind, we can begin to see that effective teaching often centers around effective living. As we strive to live pure and holy lives, other people see that in us and they begin to want to live pure and holy lives. To effectively teach others to follow Christ, we must begin by effectively learning how to follow Him ourselves.

In the end, there is a great promise here in the Great Commission: *"And surely I am with you always, to the very end of the age."* The Holy Spirit will never leave us to do the work alone. He knows the same truth that we know; we cannot get the job done on our own. He will give us the insight, the strength, the discipline, the determination, and the encouragement to carry on in this life-long journey to Christ-likeness. He also will see to it that others see His work in our lives. The Holy Spirit will draw them to see and desire His presence. As they see Him in us, they will hunger for the peace and assurance that we possess. In the end, our hope for teaching others is found in the very same place as is our hope for Heaven. God will see us through. So, let's trust Him and teach them!

Personal Thoughts:

BECOMING A LEADER

"Follow my example, as I follow the example of Christ."
(1 Corinthians 11:1)

OK, so we have talked about being a doer. It should be understood that as we accept the challenge to do something about the needs around us, these actions will change our lives. Sooner or later, as we act on the call of God and do the right things that so many others avoid, people will begin to notice. Then they will begin to follow. Before you know it, you will be a leader.

To be honest, there are those who think they are leaders, and they are not. Likewise, there are those who think they are not leaders, and they are. The difference is really quite simple. A leader is someone who leads. Now that may sound overly simple, but it really isn't. If you want to know if you are a leader, look over your shoulder. If there is anyone behind you following your example, then you are a leader. If, on the other hand, there is no one there or only people who are trying to pass you, you may not really be leading. An old Chinese proverb says, "He who thinks he leads and has no followers, is only taking a walk."

Our problem with leadership is we limit its definition to people in political or public office. This is just one type of leadership. The Apostle Paul points out to us the most fundamental and the most important type of leadership: *"Follow my example, as I follow the example of Christ."* Paul speaks here of a very personal type of leadership. It is at this personal level that leadership really makes a difference in the lives of those around us. When others can see in us a trait or habit worth emulating, and they follow our lead in that area, we have done great work.

Years ago, I had the privilege of meeting a personal hero of mine, Rev. Chuck Swindoll. He has preached literally to millions of people through his public speaking and radio ministries. He is brilliant and sincere. Upon meeting him, this is what I said: "I want to thank you for your ministry to me and ask permission to continue preaching everything I hear." At this, Chuck Swindoll laughed and replied, "Imitation is the sincerest form of flattery. You have my permission." Later, I considered that exchange and realized that this man had taught me yet another lesson. Leadership is not a matter of getting people to blindly follow your ways or accept your opinions. Leadership is learning to live and think in such a godly way that people look carefully and see a life worth emulating.

As you actively strive to live for Christ, you will become just that person. The person of the Holy Spirit will take deep root in your heart and habit, and from there He will make you a leader. Now, you may never own a company that employs hundreds of people. You may never speak from a stage to hundreds of people. You may never achieve what the world around us would call leadership. Instead, you will come to a place where you can look over your shoulder and see others, who in some small way, have patterned their lives after yours. That will make you a leader.

Personal Thoughts:

(List at least two people who have been leaders in your life and how.)

3

PRAISE

Glorifying God

WHOM I PRAISE – THE FATHER

"Come, let us sing for joy to the LORD; let us shout aloud to the Rock of our salvation. Let us come before him with thanksgiving and extol him with music and song. For the LORD is the great God, the great King above all gods. In his hand are the depths of the earth, and the mountain peaks belong to him. The sea is his, for he made it, and his hands formed the dry land. Come, let us bow down in worship, let us kneel before the LORD our Maker; for he is our God and we are the people of his pasture, the flock under his care." (Psalm 95:1-7)

The beginning place for praising God is an understanding of whom we praise. Let's be honest. We need to understand who God really is before we are going to understand the importance of praising Him. And, truth be known, we ultimately praise God simply for who He is. In this Psalm, we find five descriptions of God that help us understand why He deserves our praise.

Master – (LORD)

If you ever notice the word LORD in scripture, you may wonder why the odd capitalization? The word LORD stands for the

Hebrew word Jehovah or Yahweh. Jehovah and Yahweh are the strongest possible names for God. They represent the eternal idea of Creator, Ruler, and Master. In his encounter with the LORD, Moses found Him as the "I AM THAT I AM" (Exodus 3:14). Rather than the God who was or the God who will be, the LORD is the God who eternally IS. Always here, always in control, always present, always more than enough.

It is this God who deserves our praise simply because of who He is. We praise and revere the God of Heaven because He is Jehovah, Yahweh, and the LORD. The simple fact of the matter is our daily existence is dependent on His Sovereign will. He is the Provider of all things, the Creator of all things, the Sustainer of all things, and the Ruler of all things. He deserves our praise because He is the LORD.

Our Master deserves our Praise!

Defender – (Rock of Salvation)

In every life, there is a bit of insecurity. This also was true of King David. Although he ruled the majority of the world in which he lived, he still understood the limitations of his own power. He knew that if his enemies came against him that he would need the power of God to overcome. God, in that moment, would become the Rock of Salvation to King David and the nation of Israel. God would see them through to victory.

In our lives, we need defending as well. Though our enemies rarely charge at us with drawn swords, our lives are filled with challenges and dangers that leave us feeling a bit insecure. Just as King David, we can stand firm on God, our Rock of Salvation. He will not move beneath our feet; He is, after all, the Rock. He will not leave us to defeat; He is, after all, the Savior. Instead, He will lead us to victory as long as we remain close and committed to Him.

Our Defender deserves our Praise!

Sustainer – (In His hand)

Do you ever feel tired and alone? If you read in Psalms, you will see you are not alone. In fact, we find many heroic and courageous men and women in the Bible who came to lonely places in their lives. It is in those times that we find God never failed to sustain them. We can have faith that He will never fail to sustain us.

Just as the Psalmist paints the picture, we are held in the very hand of God. Our salvation and our future are held by the loving and powerful Almighty. There is no need for us to live in fear and uncertainty. God is with us and God will sustain us.

Our Sustainer deserves our Praise!

Creator – (LORD our Maker)

God knows us. In fact, God made us. He knows us better than we know ourselves. His loving hand has formed us and placed us here in this beautiful world He created for us. Consider the fact that God did not have to create such a beautiful place. Consider that He could have made the world cold and dark. He could have painted with dull shades of gray and hard, cold stone textures. Again, God did not have to create such a beautiful place.

From the wonderfully creative mind of God comes the vivid and glorious creation in which we live. In His mind's eye, God saw all of this. With His power, He simply spoke it into existence. All the colors, sounds, warmth, textures, emotions and passions envisioned in the mind of God were spoken into existence from the mouth of God.

Our Creator deserves our Praise!

Provider – (We are the flock under His care)

In Psalms, King David gives us a vivid image of our Providing God:

> *The LORD is my shepherd, I shall not be in want.*
> *He makes me lie down in green pastures, he leads me*
> *beside quiet waters, he restores my soul. (Psalms 23:1-3)*

In this image, we see our Great Shepherd providing the needs of His flock. God provides the necessary items for our lives. There is food and there is water for us. He leads us to places that can sustain our lives and provide our needs. Even more, He provides peace and security. The very fact that we would be comfortable enough to "*lie down in green pastures*" speaks to confidence in His protection. The waters are not troubled and rushed. Instead, they are quiet and peaceful. God has provided our needs. If we look around and have faith in Him, we will find that He also has provided our peace.

Our Provider deserves our Praise!

Personal Thoughts:

(List some things you are thankful God has provided.)

WHOM I PRAISE – THE SAVIOR

"For Christ died for sins once for all, the righteous for the unrighteous, to bring you to God. He was put to death in the body but made alive by the Spirit." (1 Peter 3:18)

Adam and Eve found themselves outside the safety and warmth of the garden, and looked ahead to a difficult, dangerous and cruel world. Their situation was a result of their own sin, and they knew it. Their lives had once been marked by long, peaceful hours in close conversation with God, and now, outside the garden, they felt very alone and very lost.

In Heaven, the heart of God was grieved, but He knew the plan. It would be costly. It would cost more than any other buyout in history. Jesus Himself, the very Son of God, would live on earth. He would live among the created beings and teach them and show them the way to the Father. In the end, He would suffer at the hands of the very people He had created. They would kill Him. The Sovereign Lord of all time would die at the hands of the creation He came to save. It seemed like an unlikely plan, and yet in the mind of God, it was done.

Jesus. The very name carries a great weight of honor and glory. His example, His teaching, His love, His forgiveness, and His sacrifice all have taught us what godliness really means. We see in His life a pattern for how we might live. We see in His death a challenge for how we might give. We see in Jesus the hope of what we might become. And yet He is so much more.

"For Christ died"

Rightly understood, the decision to salvage those of us living here on planet earth did not have to be made. It would have been an acceptable choice to simply destroy this ungrateful planet and its inhabitants and start over somewhere else. The heart of God is gracious. He decided that we were worth the price. Jesus agreed to pay the price for our sins. His blameless life would be sacrificed for our sinful souls, which would bring peace between mankind and God. Through Jesus' sacrifice, we could find forgiveness and healing for our sin-sick souls.

The only path to forgiveness for us was through the blood of a pure and spotless sacrifice. On this earth, no suitable candidate for such a sacrifice could be found. Everyone has sin. No one is blameless. Only Jesus could fill that role. By His own choice and by His own will, Jesus chose to die so that we may choose to live.

"to bring you to God"

His blood washes us clean so that we can live in a restored relationship with the Father in Heaven. In the eternal economy of Heaven, sin requires payment. Paul tells us, *"For the wages of sin is death" (Romans 6:23).* These wages are not negotiable. They are debts of sinful choices which must be paid. Without such payment, God's holy and just nature could not allow the presence of our sinful and tainted souls.

But Romans 6:23 does not stop there. It goes on to say, *"but the gift of God is eternal life in Christ Jesus our Lord."* Through the loving sacrifice of Christ Jesus, we find the gift of salvation. His blood washes us clean and makes us acceptable in the sight of God the Father. Thanks to His sacrifice, we have hope.

"He was put to death in the body but made alive by the Spirit."

The death of Jesus is not the end of the story.

If Jesus had only died for us, we would have a worthy sacrifice but not a powerful ally. You see, Jesus not only died for our sins, He rose from the dead! In His death, He won our forgiveness. In His resurrection, He has ensured us power for living. Death is a defeated enemy. Life is now the eternal future for anyone who knows the saving grace of Christ Jesus. Life here can be lived above the requirements of sin, and life eternal awaits us in Heaven with God.

Jesus lived for us, died for us, rose for us, and sits in Heaven defending us. For all this and much more, Jesus deserves our praise!

Personal Thoughts:

WHOM I PRAISE – THE SPIRIT

"But I tell you the truth: It is for your good that I am going away. Unless I go away, the Counselor will not come to you; but if I go, I will send him to you. When he comes, he will convict the world of guilt in regard to sin and righteousness and judgment: in regard to sin, because men do not believe in me; in regard to righteousness, because I am going to the Father, where you can see me no longer; and in regard to judgment, because the prince of this world now stands condemned." (John 16:7-11)

God the Father sits on the throne in Heaven. Jesus our Savior sits at His right hand defending us from the accusations of our enemy, Satan. So how are we to live here with God and Jesus there? The answer lies in the third person of the Trinity, the person of the Holy Spirit.

While many find the idea of the Holy Spirit to be uncomfortable and even strange, the truth is we need the Holy Spirit desperately in our lives. It is the person of the Holy Spirit who remains with us as we go through life. He comforts us, counsels us, leads us, and encourages us. The role of the Holy Spirit in our lives is literally to take residence in our hearts and lead us from the inside out.

"convict the world of guilt in regard to sin"

Somehow we must know when we have done wrong. That is the role of the Holy Spirit in our lives. We all can remember a time when we were about to do something that was wrong and there was that nagging sense of guilt coming from our heart. At that moment, it was an aggravation. Later, we came to understand it as that small, still voice that tells us the difference between right and wrong. Whether we listened or not, in the end, we found that the voice in our heart was right.

This voice is the voice of the Holy Spirit. He speaks to us and convicts us in regard to sin. He does not do this just to make us feel guilty. He does this to keep us on the right path. God, in His goodness, has decided that He would remind us constantly of our responsibility to do right in our lives. Through the Holy Spirit, He does just that. We may disagree, be aggravated, be angry, or even ignore the voice of the Spirit, but none of these reactions make any wrong decision right. No matter how many people we may find to agree with our opinion, it is the Holy Spirit that speaks the truth.

"convict the world of guilt in regard to ... righteousness"

Sometimes our struggle is not a matter of doing wrong things. Sometimes our struggle is more a matter of not doing right things. In these moments, the Holy Spirit will convict us in regard to righteousness. The simple fact is that God has called us to do right and to be righteous in this world. Even when the most popular and politically correct things are wrong, we are still called to do right. We are called to swim against the current of the steady stream of wrongdoing and show a confused world the right answer.

It is perhaps more common to fail to do right than it is to do wrong. We may avoid willfully doing sinful things for quite some time and still not be walking in righteousness. Righteousness requires that we not only avoid wrong but that we do right. At these times, we may argue with God and say, "But I'm not doing all of that sinful stuff anymore, God! Isn't that enough?!" The answer will be NO. It is not enough. The world does not need a list of evil actions to memorize and avoid. It needs a lifestyle of godliness to find and pursue. It is the place of the Holy Spirit to teach us this lifestyle and keep us striving to achieve a life of Christ-likeness.

It should never be forgotten that, in the end, there will be a last and final judgment. All of mankind will stand before a great throne and God will pass judgment. As we have lived, so we will be judged. As we have accepted the salvation and righteousness of God, so we will be judged. We must never forget that we all will face God and be held accountable for our actions.

The Holy Spirit will remind us of the ultimate price of sin. He will bring to our hearts and minds the reason for our lifestyle of holiness. He will remind us that we not only will be held accountable for what we have done personally, but also for how we have helped others. He will remind us that we are responsible to tell those around us about the salvation that can be found in Jesus. He will remind us that they, too, will stand before a judgment seat. If we do not warn them, they may not be prepared. If we do not tell them, they may not know. The Holy Spirit will remind us to tell them and will remind us to be ready.

For the indwelling power and the empowering work of the Holy Spirit, the Holy Spirit deserves our praise!

Personal Thoughts:

HOW I PRAISE – SACRIFICIAL PRAISE
PART 1

Some time later God tested Abraham. He said to him, "Abraham!" "Here I am," he replied. Then God said, "Take your son, your only son, Isaac, whom you love, and go to the region of Moriah. Sacrifice him there as a burnt offering on one of the mountains I will tell you about." Early the next morning Abraham got up and saddled his donkey. He took with him two of his servants and his son Isaac. When he had cut enough wood for the burnt offering, he set out for the place God had told him about. On the third day Abraham looked up and saw the place in the distance. He said to his servants, "Stay here with the donkey while I and the boy go over there. We will worship and then we will come back to you." Abraham took the wood for the burnt offering and placed it on his son Isaac, and he himself carried the fire and the knife. As the two of them went on together, Isaac spoke up and said to his father Abraham, "Father?" "Yes, my son?" Abraham replied. "The fire and wood are here," Isaac said, "but where is the lamb for the burnt offering?" Abraham answered, "God himself will provide the lamb for the burnt offering, my son." And the two of them went on together. When they reached the place God had told him about, Abraham built an altar there and arranged the wood on it. He bound his son Isaac and laid him on the altar, on top of the wood. Then he reached out his hand and took the knife to slay his son. But the angel of the LORD called out to him from heaven, "Abraham! Abraham!" "Here I am," he replied. "Do not lay a hand on the boy," he said. "Do not do anything to him. Now I know that you fear God, because you have not withheld from me your son, your only son." Abraham looked up and there in a thicket he saw a ram caught by its horns. He went over and took the ram and sacrificed it as a burnt offering instead of his son. So Abraham called that place The LORD Will Provide. And to this day it is said, "On the mountain of the LORD it will be provided." (Genesis 22:1-14)

This Biblical account can be a bit confusing. It can seem that God is uncaring and a bit cruel to even suggest that Abraham should sacrifice his son Isaac. I have seen people become angry with the fact that God would ask such a thing. However, there are lessons to be learned here. There are lessons about God, about us, and about sacrificial praise.

What do we learn about God?

Let's begin by understanding that God never intended for Abraham to sacrifice Isaac on a fiery altar. The issue here was not really about Isaac. The issue was about Abraham and his willingness to follow God in faith. We learn in Hebrews that

Abraham had full faith that God would take care of Isaac regardless of what happened on that mountain:

> *By faith Abraham, when God tested him, offered Isaac as a sacrifice. He who had received the promises was about to sacrifice his one and only son, even though God had said to him, 'It is through Isaac that your offspring will be reckoned.' Abraham reasoned that God could raise the dead, and figuratively speaking, he did receive Isaac back from death. (Hebrews 11:17-19)*

God was not calling out for the death of Isaac. He was calling out for the faith of Abraham.

The truth of the matter is that God demands our all. He expects to be the central focus of our lives and the central focus of our praise. God does not want anything to come between us and our relationship with Him. While God is jealous of our time and attention and will demand our time and attention, God is not evil and would not require, or cause, the death of a child just to get our attention.

The lesson in this account for us is one of priority. God is, and must be recognized as, the top priority in our lives. We cannot allow anything else to take His place at the top of our priority list. We must keep Him first. This is not due to some self-centered need on the part of God. This is because of who He really is. If it is true that God is the King of the Universe, and He is, then it must also be true that He is the most important relationship we have. When we see Him as our top priority, we can worship Him with proper perspective, proper honor, and proper glory.

Personal Thoughts:

(Have you allowed anything to come between you and your relationship with God?)

HOW I PRAISE – SACRIFICIAL PRAISE
PART 2

Some time later God tested Abraham. He said to him, "Abraham!" "Here I am," he replied. Then God said, "Take your son, your only son, Isaac, whom you love, and go to the region of Moriah. Sacrifice him there as a burnt offering on one of the mountains I will tell you about." Early the next morning Abraham got up and saddled his donkey. He took with him two of his servants and his son Isaac. When he had cut enough wood for the burnt offering, he set out for the place God had told him about. On the third day Abraham looked up and saw the place in the distance. He said to his servants, "Stay here with the donkey while I and the boy go over there. We will worship and then we will come back to you." Abraham took the wood for the burnt offering and placed it on his son Isaac, and he himself carried the fire and the knife. As the two of them went on together, Isaac spoke up and said to his father Abraham, "Father?" "Yes, my son?" Abraham replied. "The fire and wood are here," Isaac said, "but where is the lamb for the burnt offering?" Abraham answered, "God himself will provide the lamb for the burnt offering, my son." And the two of them went on together. When they reached the place God had told him about, Abraham built an altar there and arranged the wood on it. He bound his son Isaac and laid him on the altar, on top of the wood. Then he reached out his hand and took the knife to slay his son. But the angel of the LORD called out to him from heaven, "Abraham! Abraham!" "Here I am," he replied. "Do not lay a hand on the boy," he said. "Do not do anything to him. Now I know that you fear God, because you have not withheld from me your son, your only son." Abraham looked up and there in a thicket he saw a ram caught by its horns. He went over and took the ram and sacrificed it as a burnt offering instead of his son. So Abraham called that place The LORD Will Provide. And to this day it is said, "On the mountain of the LORD it will be provided." (Genesis 22:1-14)

Same story, but let's consider it from a different angle. We already have considered what we could learn about God from this encounter. Now, let's consider what we can learn about us.

Honestly, as humans we are quite fickle. One day we are focused on one thing, and the next day we are focused on another. At one time in our lives we believe in one truth, and at another time in our lives we accept something else. We jump from priority to priority and often show little concern for the effect this wavering has on others. Worse yet, in our leaping from one priority to another, we often miss the truly important and replace it with the latest fad.

Now, don't get me wrong, there are some very important things in our lives that we focus on from time to time. Things like our spouse, our children, our work, our ministry, our future and so on. None of these are bad things, and all of them require our attention. However, none of them can be allowed to take the place of God. In our lives, only one can sit on the throne, and that must be God Himself.

When we allow anything else on the throne of our lives, we set ourselves up for disappointment and failure. You see, God is the only thing that will never change and never fail. Everything and everyone else in our lives will come and go, but God will always remain. When our marriages face death or divorce, God is still there. When our children break our hearts, God is still there. When our careers stall or even end, God is still there. When our ministry fails to succeed, God is still there. When our future seems bleak and unclear, God is still there. At every turn and in every circumstance, we always can count on God to be unchanging in His love for us and unshaken in His commitment to us. God will always be there.

This explains why He must be on the ultimate throne of our lives. The person or thing we allow on that throne determines our stability, our hope, and our future. While we love and trust those around us, they will change and at times they will fail. God will not. While we work hard and focus on our careers and our ministry, these may fail. God will not. Should the moment come when the entire world around us begins to crumble, God will still be on His throne. He will remain steady and strong. He will hold us steady, if we leave Him in charge.

The throne of our hearts and lives is built for the King of Heaven. It is truly unsuited for anyone or anything else.

Personal Thoughts:

HOW I PRAISE – SACRIFICIAL PRAISE
PART 3

"Then they called them in again and commanded them not to speak or teach at all in the name of Jesus. But Peter and John replied, 'Judge for yourselves whether it is right in God's sight to obey you rather than God. For we cannot help speaking about what we have seen and heard.'" (Acts 4:18-20)

In the early church, it was always understood that being a believer in Christ Jesus was hazardous to your health. The early church was challenged from every side by those who wanted to destroy it. The Romans feared an uprising of those who would follow the memory of this self-proclaimed "King" named Jesus. The Jews understood that Jesus' claim to being the Messiah was a real threat to their way of life and their spiritual authority. The merchants of the day were making great amounts of money selling trinkets to the pagan worshippers. All of these people had a personal interest in seeing this infant church fail.

Therefore, many of the early church leaders found themselves spending time in prison. They were beaten, threatened, and eventually killed for their faith. History and tradition tell us that all but one of the disciples died a violent death defending their faith with their last breath. John, who died of old age, spent much of his life in exile on a forsaken prison island called Patmos. In short, their faith cost them something. In reality, their faith cost them everything. Their praise was sacrificial.

It is no coincidence that the early church movement, so marked with pain and suffering, also was marked by great miracles of God. He saw the suffering of His people and He responded with the miraculous. People were healed and demons were sent running. This church, under siege, grew dramatically. God moved on behalf of people who were willing to give their all for His best!

What about us? What has our faith cost us? We struggle reading the account of Abraham and Isaac. How could we ever have faith that deep? Instead, we not only seem to have a faith that is not deep, but at times it seems cheap. We search for comfortable sanctuaries, easy listening sermons, and fun activities. We stay home on rainy Sundays, stay in bed with a slight sniffle, and avoid moments that may prove challenging. Our faith has not cost us much at all. In return, it does not produce much at all.

Praise should cost us something. Perhaps you have participated in some type of prayer and fasting, which are wonderful learning experiences. For you, faith is costing something. You have decided to restrict yourself from some comfort in order to give praise to God. The lesson in that practice is invaluable. In our culture, faith rarely requires real sacrifice on our part. We are given the freedom to worship, preach and teach the great Gospel of Christ, and for this freedom we should be grateful. We also should take care that our freedom does not cause us to be complacent.

Perhaps the most dangerous enemy to the Gospel is comfort. Too much comfort can make us soft. Too much comfort can make us unwilling to stand for our faith when doing so is painful or difficult. Too much comfort can rob us of the depths of our faith and commitment and leave us incapable of experiencing the miraculous work of God in our daily lives. We should search for ways to move out of our comfort zones and into the richness of God's blessings!

So ask yourself: "What does my faith cost me? Do I give of myself to others? Do I give of my time to God and His church? Do I give of my money as God has called me to? Do I take risks by speaking of His goodness and grace? What does my faith cost me?" Keep in mind as you ask yourself these questions what it cost Christ. He died so that we might live in His grace and peace. So, what are you willing to give to the One who gave you so much?

Personal Thoughts:

HOW I PRAISE – HEALING PRAISE

Now Naaman was commander of the army of the king of Aram. He was a great man in the sight of his master and highly regarded, because through him the LORD had given victory to Aram. He was a valiant soldier, but he had leprosy.... So Naaman went with his horses and chariots and stopped at the door of Elisha's house. Elisha sent a messenger to say to him, "Go, wash yourself seven times in the Jordan, and your flesh will be restored and you will be cleansed." But Naaman went away angry and said, "I thought that he would surely come out to me and stand and call on the name of the LORD his God, wave his hand over the spot and cure me of my leprosy. Are not Abana and Pharpar, the rivers of Damascus, better than any of the waters of Israel? Couldn't I wash in them and be cleansed?" So he turned and went off in a rage. Naaman's servants went to him and said, "My father, if the prophet had told you to do some great thing, would you not have done it? How much more, then, when he tells you, 'Wash and be cleansed'!" So he went down and dipped himself in the Jordan seven times, as the man of God had told him, and his flesh was restored and became clean like that of a young boy. (2 Kings 5:1, 9-14)

There is a healing aspect to worship. In fact, it is often in the process of faithfully worshipping God that we find His miraculous healing presence.

Naaman was a man who believed in God but almost missed God's healing in his life. Naaman was an important man. He was well connected and successful, but like many of us he faced a situation that was beyond his control. Naaman understood that he was not able to heal himself. He did not struggle with false feelings of superiority when it came to healing. He knew that healing was God's area and he needed God's help. Naaman's struggle was with his expectations of how God would do His job of healing.

Naaman went to the Prophet Elisha and expected to be greeted as the important dignitary that he knew he was. He was waiting for the red carpet treatment and for a Prophet who would relish the opportunity to call down the blessings of his God for a man of such prominence. However, that is not at all what happened. Elisha was not impressed by Naaman's position or his importance. Elisha understood that the only dignitary in this proceeding was going to be God Himself. God would do this in His own way and He alone would get the glory. God would teach Naaman a lesson.

So there Naaman stood, his entourage at his side, waiting at the door for the Prophet to rush out to meet him. Instead, a servant opened the door and said, *"Go, wash yourself seven times in the Jordan, and your flesh will be restored and you will be cleansed" (2 Kings 5:10).* Then the servant went back inside and the door was closed. Naaman must have thought: "That's it?! He did not even come out and speak to me! He sent a servant with a message and did not even bother to meet me?!" Naaman was furious.

Let's pause here. How many times have we expected God to act in a certain manner and have been angered when He did not? You see, God is not impressed by our self-importance. He is not concerned with our sense of fairness or our sense of respect we think we deserve. He is interested in our understanding of a real need for Him. He will not feed our over-inflated egos. He instead will establish His overwhelming power.

So the command was given: *"Go, wash yourself seven times in the Jordan,"* which, again, infuriated Naaman. *"Are not Abana and Pharpar, the rivers of Damascus, better than any of the waters of Israel? Couldn't I wash in them and be cleansed?" (2 Kings 5:10, 12).* The answer to this question was a resounding NO! God said to wash in the Jordan River, and not once but seven times. This water seemed beneath the dignity of Naaman, yet it is what God had said to do.

Initially, Naaman refused. His anger got the best of him and he simply would not be reduced to seven dips in that nasty river, but his servants encouraged him to go ahead. God had not required anything difficult or great of him, only a long bath in a dirty river. So Naaman finally agreed, and when he gave God the place of priority over his own preferences, Naaman found healing.

Praising God, on God's terms, can bring great healing into our lives. We are, after all, His creation and His people. God's healing presence is often found in our submissive praise.

Personal Thoughts:

4

ACTION

Fulfilling physical, emotional, and spiritual needs through Biblical truth applied in Christian love

FULFILLING
PART 1

"For I know the plans I have for you,' declares the LORD, 'plans to prosper you and not to harm you, plans to give you hope and a future.'" (Jeremiah 29:11)

God made us for a purpose. While that truth is well established in most minds, the implications of it are often overlooked. The very fact that God has a plan for every life gives meaning and purpose to our existence. It gives direction to our decisions and strengthens our resolve. God made you for a purpose.

The fact we were made for a purpose also teaches us that we were made for work. We were not made to sit around and accomplish little to nothing in this world.

Our family had a dog named Frodo. Frodo was created to sit around and do a lot of nothing. His only purpose in life was to play with our children and sit quietly on our laps while we scratched his ears. Not a very tough assignment in life if you ask me. Frodo could sleep for upwards of 15 hours per day. The dog would play for a couple of hours and then sleep for a couple more.

He was designed by God, not for work, but for companionship.

It may seem that Frodo had a wonderful life. We might even think that we would like to be able to sleep half the day and play the other half. The problem is we are not created like Frodo. We were created to accomplish things in our lives and God skilled us for the very accomplishments He wants to see out of us. He has given us purpose and we need to accept it.

Fulfillment, rightly understood, is working within the purpose that God has for our lives. God created you to be fulfilled, not frustrated! Frustration comes when we fail to recognize or exercise the purpose of God for our lives.

Recognizing my Purpose

So many times people seem to believe that God must mean for them to do something that they will hate doing. They fully expect to be called to a life or place that will be difficult for them to accept and virtually miserable for them to live. Many times we seem to wonder, "Service can't be fun, can it?" The answer is a resounding YES! Think about it. If God created you for a specific purpose, and He skilled you to accomplish that purpose, and then He gave you the desire to pursue that purpose, then doesn't it stand to reason that you would enjoy doing what it is God desires for you?

Sometimes we fail to see the importance of the work we do. It is easy to look around and see others doing the "really important" tasks while we are just doing the "small stuff." The truth is there is no "small stuff." Everything we do for God's Kingdom makes a big difference.

While I was a teen in North Carolina, I attended First Wesleyan Church in Kannapolis. I learned a great deal there and remember many of the people who made a difference in my life during those years. However, there was one lady who I always looked forward to seeing on Sunday mornings. Mrs. Haithcock would greet me every Sunday with a big smile and hug. Every week, I knew that when I walked into that church, Mrs. Haithcock would be there and she would be glad to see me. Her job was simple: she was to love people. Her importance was immeasurable. She made me feel important and loved. In God's Kingdom, there really is no "small stuff."

Exercising my Purpose

When I was about 20 years old, I really began to wrestle with the idea that I might be called to ministry. It seemed that the gifts were there and the desire to minister from the pulpit was growing, but I wasn't certain. I knew I needed a special call from God and I was not sure how to recognize that call. I sat down with a pastor friend and talked with him about my dilemma. I will always remember what he said: "Mike, stop looking for a lightning bolt and start ministering." In other words, spend less time questioning and more time working.

You will find it much easier to discover your skills by working than by studying. In fact, you can study for years about any given work and never know if you have the skills to excel. You have to work at it to find out if you are good at it. Unfortunately, church people can spend so much time talking about doing something that they lack the time to actually get something done.

If you think you may be skilled at something, try it. The worst that can happen is that you will fail. With God, failure is not final; it is only part of the learning process. Get in there and exercise the gifts and skills you have and you will better understand what God's purpose is for your life.

In the end, we look for an area of work that fulfills us. I describe fulfillment in work this way: When I would do what I do even if they did not pay me to do it, that is fulfilling!

Personal Thoughts:

FULFILLING

PART 2

"They came to Capernaum. When he was in the house, he asked them, 'What were you arguing about on the road?' But they kept quiet because on the way they had argued about who was the greatest. Sitting down, Jesus called the Twelve and said, 'If anyone wants to be first, he must be the very last, and the servant of all.'" (Mark 9:33-35)

We live in a self-centered culture. We have been taught that happiness and fulfillment come from wealth and material possessions. We see people around us constantly striving to get something they do not have believing that this one thing will bring true happiness. "If I just had the right car … a better house … better clothes … a better diet … a better job …" On and on that list can go. The truth is, we don't need better stuff in our lives. We need a better purpose for our lives.

Jesus understood and modeled a different truth. Here we find the very King and Creator of the universe living among and serving His creation. Jesus, God, was found healing the sick, feeding the hungry, teaching the curious, leading the lost, comforting the sorrowful, honoring the children, and washing the feet of His disciples. Jesus knew that true personal fulfillment is only found in service to others.

The way that God has designed us is both interesting and brilliant. He knew that we, like the disciples, would debate and argue over who is the greatest. He understood that we would each want to be seen as the most important, most talented, most popular, and most powerful in our own circles. He designed us in such a way that those awards and titles are really not that fulfilling. He designed us to find fulfillment only in fulfilling relationships with others. God has forced us to serve one another in order to find true peace and happiness.

Our purpose in life should always be focused on other people. We will be called to help others. Whether it is feeding the hungry, teaching the curious, healing the sick, helping the feeble, comforting the sorrowful or leading the lost, we are called to help make someone's life better. We must look beyond ourselves in order to find the deepest meaning and purpose for our lives.

Unfortunately, our culture, even our church culture, is self-focused. We talk about MY prayer life, MY spiritual gifts, MY struggles, MY giving,

MY God, MY Savior, MY church, and MY ministry. We focus on what is ours (personal) instead of what is ours (corporate). That self-centered focus is not only unhealthy, it is not godly. It will not help us find meaning and purpose.

If we are to learn from Jesus on this matter of finding fulfillment, we must see in His life the heart of a servant. The Ruler of the universe was the greatest servant ever. He came to this earth to die for our sins. He submitted Himself to that punishment and humiliation not because it was what He wanted, but because it was what we needed. He came to serve and He showed us how to serve.

So, rightly understood, this changes the basic question in our lives. Most of us have spent our time wondering, "What will make my life better?" Instead we should be asking, "How can I make others' lives better?" And somehow, in the beauty of how God made us, answering that question will make our lives better and more fulfilling.

Personal Thoughts:

PHYSICAL NEED

"What good is it, my brothers, if a man claims to have faith but has no deeds? Can such faith save him? Suppose a brother or sister is without clothes and daily food. If one of you says to him, 'Go, I wish you well; keep warm and well fed,' but does nothing about his physical needs, what good is it? In the same way, faith by itself, if it is not accompanied by action, is dead. But someone will say, 'You have faith; I have deeds.' Show me your faith without deeds, and I will show you my faith by what I do." (James 2:14-18)

We are saved by faith alone, but not faith that is alone. That statement has been used for centuries to explain the often misunderstood relationship between faith and works. While it is true that we cannot earn our salvation by any amount of works, it is also true that a person who has come to know the saving grace of Jesus Christ will do the good work of his Savior.

Our faith is all about becoming more like Jesus. Becoming the best possible example of His holiness and righteousness is the ultimate goal of our Christianity. This process of becoming requires action. If we are really to become like Christ, we must be busy doing the servant work He modeled for us.

James asks a profound question in this scripture: *"What good is it, my brothers, if a man claims to have faith but has no deeds? Can such faith save him?"* The obvious implication of this question is no; faith without deeds is not a saving faith. Faith that is real is also faith that is working. A real faith is a serving faith. A real Christian is a servant of others. It is our job to find some way to help and serve those around us. We must be looking for needs, caring about needs, and helping to fill those needs.

An Observant Servant

To start with, we must work at seeing the needs around us. This means that we must stop focusing on ourselves and start paying attention to others. Most of us are so involved in our own sense of neediness that we simply fail to see the needs of other people. We may care, but we just don't notice. James 2:15 says, *"Suppose a brother or sister is without clothes and daily food."* The obvious assumption is that we would notice those who are in need.

Needs take many forms. There is the need for clothing, food and shelter that obviously come to mind. Christians must be about the business of working to fill those needs. However, there are many other needs. There is the need for friendship and fellowship, mentoring and leadership, and comfort and understanding. The list can go on and on. Needs may be as complex as life-long care or as simple as a smile and a warm greeting. No matter what the need, it cannot be met if it is not recognized.

A Compassionate Servant

James then addresses our response to the needs that we have seen:

> *Suppose a brother or sister is without clothes and daily food. If one of you says to him, 'Go, I wish you well; keep warm and well fed,' but does nothing about his physical needs, what good is it? In the same way, faith by itself, if it is not accompanied by action, is dead. (James 2:15-17)*

Noticing a need does no good if we are not willing to act on filling that need.

Far too often we simply offer to pray for those in need and take no action. Honestly, that is nothing more than a spiritualized cop-out. We are hiding our unwillingness to help behind a spiritual facade of prayer. Now, I do not want to underestimate the power of prayer; I simply want it to be in balance with the very real Biblical call to action. Pray for those in need! Then consider the fact that God's answer to their need just might be you.

An Involved Servant

There is another spiritualized excuse: *"But someone will say, 'You have faith; I have deeds'" (James 2:18).* Yet again, a spiritual way to say: "I just really don't care enough to get involved." This type of inaction is not acceptable to God. Our Father expects us to help when we can and to be involved in the lives of others. He expects us to step up and speak with James when he says, *"Show me your faith without deeds, and I will show you my faith by what I do" (James 2:18).* So, do something for God. Do something in the church. Do something in the workplace. Do something in the neighborhood. Do something in the political arena. Do something in the schools. Just find a need and do something about it.

Now some will argue that there is not enough time to get involved. Well, let's put that to rest quickly. We make time to do what we deem to be important. I don't doubt that we all have busy schedules and over-worked lives, but we also have the freedom to choose what we will do with our time. Will we choose to make time for compassionate service, or will we choose to ignore the call of our compassionate heart? Either way, it is our choice. Just remember when He thought of us and our need for forgiveness, Jesus chose compassion.

Personal Thoughts:

EMOTIONAL NEED

"All his brothers and sisters and everyone who had known him before came and ate with him in his house. They comforted and consoled him over all the trouble the LORD had brought upon him, and each one gave him a piece of silver and a gold ring." (Job 42:11)

The most difficult times in our lives are times of emotional distress. In moments of great personal loss or deep depression, we need the help, support and comfort of others more than ever. We may survive physical needs on our own and we may find answers to spiritual needs through a personal search, but emotional needs require other people.

Job learned this lesson the hard way. In the Old Testament, we find an entire book on the life of Job. The book of Job is admittedly not the most uplifting of stories. It is, in fact, a little disturbing. It seems that God allowed Satan to take everything away from Job. His family, his wealth, and his health were all gone in a matter of hours. From being a man of considerable wealth and honor, he found himself sitting in a pile of ashes scratching sores that had appeared all over his body. Life had

truly gone bad for Job, and he needed some
support.

Unfortunately, the first people to show up
were not much help. Job's wife gave some advice
that was not really helpful: *"Are you still holding on to
your integrity? Curse God and die!" (Job 2:9)*. If that
wasn't enough, he had some "friends" show up.
They accused him of some hidden sin that must
have caused this trouble to come his way. Surely
Job must have done some horrible thing in order
for all of this to take place. The truth is Job had
done nothing wrong.

Finally, after 40+ chapters of bad and painful
advice, some truly compassionate people show up.
These people were Job's real friends and family.
They ministered to him and helped him through a
terrible time. The lesson here is that we should
learn how to minister to those who find themselves
in the grips of a painful and emotional struggle.

A Ministry of Presence

*"All his brothers and sisters and everyone who had known
him before came and ate with him in his house. They
comforted and consoled him over all the trouble the LORD
had brought upon him."*

There is great power in just showing up. Often during emotional crises, words fail. What matters in these moments is not what someone says; what matters is that someone is there. Someone who will sit with you, cry with you, remember with you, laugh with you, and pray with you. Even when the prayers are painful, by someone else just simply being there can make these moments easier to bear.

Some years ago Tina's dad, J. Allen, felt the call to go in to ministry. Her mom, Debbie, did not feel that she had any useful gifts for ministry. She was born in South Korea and had some language barriers and felt insecure about her ability to minister. I assured her that she would have no trouble. I had observed her working with people in the church that I pastored. I had watched her stand beside people who were discouraged or depressed and just be there with them. I had watched her walk through a receiving line at the funeral home hugging each family member and crying with them in their time of sorrow. I had seen her spend hours cooking for people who needed a little extra cheer during a holiday season or a time of sickness. She naturally understood a ministry of presence.

A Ministry of Giving

"and each one gave him a piece of silver and a gold ring."

Sometimes people need more than our presence. Sometimes they need our presents. Now, it is true that not everyone who asks for money or food is really in need or worthy of our help. However, it is also true that there are times when hard-working, well-meaning, God-fearing men and women find themselves in a moment of need that cannot be dealt with alone. At that time, we must remember the giving spirit of our Lord Jesus and come to their aid.

Giving in this manner is not a matter of a hand-out; it is a hand-up. Job's friends and family were saying: "We believe in you and we are willing to invest in your future." They were doing more than just offering to pray. They were offering to pay some of the bills until Job could get back on his feet. This is an investment in a friend.

In 1998, it seemed that New Life Church might go under. Money was extremely tight and the bills were large and late. During this time, the Chesapeake District of the Wesleyan Church decided to invest in a family member. They helped pay the bills and helped fund ministry until things could get better. This was no welfare move; this was an investment in the future. And boy, did it pay off! Today, New Life Church is the largest single contributor to the funding of the Chesapeake District. Simply put, tough times do not indicate a lack of value. They just indicate tough times.

The investment that Job's friends made in him paid off as well:

> *The LORD blessed the latter part of Job's life more than the first. He had fourteen thousand sheep, six thousand camels, a thousand yoke of oxen and a thousand donkeys. And he also had seven sons and three daughters. The first daughter he named Jemimah, the second Keziah and the third Keren-Happuch. Nowhere in all the land were there found women as beautiful as Job's daughters, and their father granted them an inheritance along with their brothers. After this, Job lived a hundred and forty years; he saw his children and their children to the fourth generation. And so he died, old and full of years. (Job 42:12-17)*

Emotional need does not mean the end of a successful life. It simply calls for the emotional support of people who choose to believe in you, no matter what.

Personal Thoughts:

SPIRITUAL NEED

*"Do not be anxious about anything, but in everything, by prayer and petition, with thanksgiving, present your requests to God. And the peace of God, which transcends all understanding, will guard your hearts and your minds in Christ Jesus. Finally, brothers, whatever is true, whatever is noble, whatever is right, whatever is pure, whatever is lovely, whatever is admirable – if anything is excellent or praiseworthy – think about such things. Whatever you have learned or received or heard from me, or seen in me – put it into practice. And the God of peace will be with you."
(Philippians 4:6-9)*

Most of us really do want to help others. However, our attempts often seem ineffective or unappreciated. The problem is not our motivation or our information. The problem is our focus. You see, most people, even professionals, work hard at dealing with the symptoms of our problems and never take the time to understand the core of our problems. They would see that as too difficult or complex an issue to even attempt to understand, when in reality it's not so difficult at all.

You see, all of our problems really stem from one source = sin. Sin causes a lack of right perspective, a lack of right desire, and a lack of right actions. This lack of right thinking and right acting has some consequences. Sin always has consequences, and over time, these sinful actions begin to pile up massive consequences. These consequences become the symptoms that most people work to address. For example, a consequence of gambling could be poverty. A consequence of promiscuous sexual activity could be disease, unplanned pregnancy or divorce. A consequence of drinking alcohol could be loss of income, relationships, and even life. A consequence of lying could be loss of relationships and trust. All of the actions that the sin in our lives would lead us to have consequences and cause problems.

While dealing with the symptoms, or consequences of sin, may seem like the greatest need at that moment, what really needs to be dealt with is the pattern of wrong decisions. Destructive decisions destroy lives. Therefore, if you really want to change your life or help someone else change theirs, you have to change your focus and your actions.

A Change in Focus

Before coming to know Christ and

understanding His call to holy living, we tend to focus on our own feelings and desires. Our focus is inward and self-centered. We are concerned with personal wants, feelings and desires and can virtually ignore the deeper questions of right and wrong. Christ calls us to change all of that.

In this scripture, we find the Apostle Paul writing to the church in Philippi:

> *Do not be anxious about anything, but in everything, by prayer and petition, with thanksgiving, present your requests to God. And the peace of God, which transcends all understanding, will guard your hearts and your minds in Christ Jesus. (Philippians 4:6-7)*

Paul is calling them to change the way they look at the world around them. Up to this point, they have focused on themselves and found that this left them feeling anxious and worried. Paul instructs them to change their focus to God. This change in focus has some profound effects.

When we place our focus on God through prayer, we are able to put our problems into perspective. We can see them in light of the awesome God we serve. This makes our problems seem smaller because in comparison to God, they are; then they seem more manageable. We also find ourselves reminded of all that God has done for us. This takes an anxious moment and introduces the calming effect of thankfulness. In the end, we remember that we can take our problems to God and leave them there. He will help us through. He may not snap His divine fingers and make them all go away, but He will be there to help and to heal.

Paul does not simply tell us to focus on God; he gives us a practical list of qualities to look for and to direct our focus:

> *Finally, brothers, whatever is true, whatever is noble, whatever is right, whatever is pure, whatever is lovely, whatever is admirable – if anything is excellent or praiseworthy – think about such things. (Philippians 4:8)*

This list of qualities can become a matrix through which you can judge the choices you make. Whether it is a movie, a website, a song, a party, a photo or a friend, this can become a checklist for making right choices.

A Change in Action

"Whatever you have learned or received or heard from me, or seen in me – put it into practice. And the God of peace will be with you."

Now that we have a new focus and a new checklist of right qualities, we have the ability to make new and better decisions. We can put in to practice everything God has commanded of us. Right actions, just like sinful ones, have consequences. The only difference is that right actions have positive consequences. God has given us the ability to live a new life. A new life that is free from the guilt and penalty of sin. He has made it possible for us to change our thoughts and actions so that instead of guilt, we can find blessings!

Personal Thoughts:

BIBLICAL TRUTH APPLIED IN CHRISTIAN LOVE

"This is how we know what love is: Jesus Christ laid down his life for us. And we ought to lay down our lives for our brothers. If anyone has material possessions and sees his brother in need but has no pity on him, how can the love of God be in him? Dear children, let us not love with words or tongue but with actions and in truth." (1 John 3:16-18)

Let us love *"with actions and in truth."* John spells it out well. The love of Christ in us compels us to act when we see others in need. The Holy Spirit Himself will tug at our hearts so that we will know that the time for service is here. God expects us to minister to those in need, but there is more to it than just helping others. We are called to help people find the truth of the Bible as we work with them. We are to show them that there is more in this world than just varying opinion. There is a real, absolute truth that comes to us from a great and loving God.

The problem many Christians face is that they focus on either the compassion or the truth. Either, alone, are not effective in leading people to better decisions and therefore better actions. Simply put, compassionate help without Biblical truth is shallow and its benefits are short-lived. Biblical truth without compassionate love is difficult and harsh. Both are required. While compassionate love is very attractive to those in need, it is the truth that gives us a pattern for living that allows true life change.

Now some would argue that there is no absolute truth that can be known and applied. They would argue that the Bible is just another book filled with great ideas and philosophies. They would simply equate the Bible with any other sacred writing from any other religious tradition. Yet God does not see it that way. The Bible makes it clear that truth is of utmost importance. In fact, the word truth itself appears 118 times in the New Testament alone. God sees truth as important.

Truth is also effective. In writing to Timothy, the Apostle Paul reminds him that:

> *All Scripture is God-breathed and is useful for teaching, rebuking, correcting and training in righteousness, so that the man of God may be thoroughly equipped for every good work. (2 Timothy 3:16-17)*

Biblical truth is always effective at changing the

lives of those who are willing to hear and apply it.

While Biblical truth requires right living, Christian love requires compassion. Jesus showed us compassion throughout His life on earth. His greatest display of compassion came on the cross. He knew that we needed this ultimate sacrifice in order to find forgiveness. He understood that we could not just overcome sinfulness on our own and that the price of our sin had to be paid. Jesus, on the cross, displayed the ultimate compassion for the entire human race.

We need to take the entire example of Jesus and apply it to our own lives. Resist the desire to focus on compassion or truth. Remember that both are required if we are to reach a lost and needy world with a faith that is both loving and life-changing.

Personal Thoughts:

GO …

"But you, keep your head in all situations, endure hardship, do the work of an evangelist, discharge all the duties of your ministry." (2 Timothy 4:5)

So, we are called to action. God expects us to be doing something about the faith that He has given us. He expects us to be busy about the work of His Kingdom. He expects us to be reaching those who do not know Him. In 2 Timothy, the Apostle Paul is writing his last letter during what he knows will be his final days. In the letter, he gives some instruction to his young pastor that can be helpful to us.

Stay Focused

"But you, keep your head in all situations"

Paul knew there would be many difficult situations ahead for young Timothy. He knew that Satan would send distractions and difficulties to shake the faith and effectiveness of the church and its leaders. Paul knew they would have to remain level-headed.

Likewise, in our lives, Satan will send distractions to take us away from the important work of reaching the world for Christ. These distractions are not always bad things in and of themselves. Often we would consider them blessings, but they distract us from the work of the Kingdom nonetheless.

Sometimes Satan will distract us by causing us to question the importance of our contribution. During these times, we find ourselves asking some difficult questions. What is the point of all this work? Why should I care so much when no one else does? What good am I doing anyway? These questions are only distractions, sent from Satan to keep us off balance. The truth is that we could find nothing more important than our work for the Kingdom of God. Serving God through His church is one of the most important things we can do.

Stay Tough

"endure hardship"

Satan also will send difficulties. He will send people and situations to hit us from every angle. It will seem like we are the most unlucky or un-liked people in the world, and yet it is only a tactic of the devil to keep us from being effective. His goal is to keep you as ineffective in reaching people for Christ as possible, so he will take some difficult people and send them your way.

Don't let difficult people slow you down. They are most often not right in their complaints. In order to move on with confidence, follow this simple plan:

1. Honestly consider your motives – if you are doing things for the right reasons, move on!
2. Honestly consider your process – if you are doing things in right and fair ways, move on!
3. Honestly consider your progress – if God is giving you success, move on!

When in this process you find problems that are really yours, deal with them immediately, ask for forgiveness from the proper people, and move on!

Stay Evangelistic

"do the work of an evangelist"

The only reason for the existence of the church is to reach the world with the saving grace of Jesus Christ! If you are doing ministry for any other reason, you are missing the point. Our goal is to bring people into the Kingdom of God under the saving blood of Jesus. Everything we do, everything we say, and every plan we make should have this one, simple goal.

Stay Busy

"discharge all the duties of your ministry"

I know that the last thing we need is another reason to stay busy. I understand that what most of us want is a chance to slow down and do less, but we have to keep eternity in mind. There are people all around us who will slip away without the hope of salvation unless we continue to do the work of ministry that God has given us. While it is never good for us to over-work and burn ourselves out, it is important that we stay at the task. Whatever it takes, remember this, people truly need the Good News of Salvation, and God has given us the privilege of spreading that Good News.

Therefore, GO!

Personal Thoughts:

5

CALLING

Going to reach the world for Christ

HEAR THE CALL

"Now Moses was tending the flock of Jethro his father-in-law, the priest of Midian, and he led the flock to the far side of the desert and came to Horeb, the mountain of God. There the angel of the LORD appeared to him in flames of fire from within a bush. Moses saw that though the bush was on fire it did not burn up. So Moses thought, 'I will go over and see this strange sight – why the bush does not burn up.' When the LORD saw that he had gone over to look, God called to him from within the bush, 'Moses! Moses!' And Moses said, 'Here I am.'" (Exodus 3:1-4)

The people of God were held captive in a country that once offered them refuge from famine and starvation. What had once been a place of protection and comfort had become a place of captivity. The answer to their prayers was tending sheep in the desert. God always seems to work that way. His answers often seem the least likely and the least possible. The people He chooses to use are rarely the ones we would have chosen. Instead, they are damaged and seemingly ruined individuals.

But God's call makes all the difference. In Exodus 3, Moses' very existence is about to change. He will begin his day as a shepherd of sheep that are not even his. He will end this day as the hope of a nation who will respect his faith and courage for thousands of years to come. The difference? God's call.

"Now Moses was tending the flock of Jethro his father-in-law, the priest of Midian, and he led the flock to the far side of the desert and came to Horeb, the mountain of God. There the angel of the LORD appeared to him in flames of fire from within a bush. Moses saw that though the bush was on fire it did not burn up. So Moses thought, 'I will go over and see this strange sight – why the bush does not burn up.'"

God will often reveal Himself in the mundane ritual of daily life. Perhaps you find yourself in a place where you cannot really sense a clear call of God on your life and you are wondering what you should do now. The answer is to keep doing what you know is right. Moses was born to be a leader, but at that moment, he was simply a shepherd. He spent his days tending to sheep that belonged to his father-in-law Jethro. Moses' career path did not seem to be upwardly mobile.

It is in the mundane ritual of life that we develop our commitment to doing the right things. In the small moments of temptation and victory, we develop character. When we refuse to cheat on a test, or to take an extra 20 minutes on break, or to blame our failure on someone else, we develop the righteous habits of living that God can use so powerfully. It is in the small things that God prepares us to deal with the big things.

Until you see a clear call, just keep doing the right thing. God has not forgotten you. He is building you, and using you in ways that you may not see. Trust in His divine will and He will show you the way.

"So Moses thought, 'I will go over and see this strange sight – why the bush does not burn up.' When the LORD saw that he had gone over to look, God called to him from within the bush, 'Moses! Moses!' And Moses said, 'Here I am.'"

The most important ability that God is looking for in all of us is avail-ability. God wants us to be available for His work and His call. Unfortunately, we often are not willing to do the work of making ourselves available. We run from the hard work and frustration of change and even ignore the obvious, burning bush, road signs that God would use to lead us in a new direction. For some reason, many of us resist God's leadership in our lives.

I think one of the key reasons for this resistance of God's will is a lack of trust in God's love. We know, in our heads, God loves us and wants the best for us, but we lack the faith in our hearts to trust that love when the call is difficult and the task seems impossible. This is a lack of faith. God has always used people who were under-educated, under-funded, under-appreciated, and under pressure. God has always used people like us. Normal people. Folks who have spent most of their lives getting up early in the morning and heading off to a job we find bearable and a world we find survivable, are the very people God loves to take to new and unheard-of levels of achievement.

He can take you there, if, when He calls, you are ready to listen and ready to go.

Personal Thoughts:

ACCEPT THE CHALLENGE

"'Do not come any closer,' God said. 'Take off your sandals, for the place where you are standing is holy ground.' Then he said, 'I am the God of your father, the God of Abraham, the God of Isaac and the God of Jacob.' At this, Moses hid his face, because he was afraid to look at God. The LORD said, 'I have indeed seen the misery of my people in Egypt. I have heard them crying out because of their slave drivers, and I am concerned about their suffering. So I have come down to rescue them from the hand of the Egyptians and to bring them up out of that land into a good and spacious land, a land flowing with milk and honey – the home of the Canaanites, Hittites, Amorites, Perizzites, Hivites and Jebusites. And now the cry of the Israelites has reached me, and I have seen the way the Egyptians are oppressing them. So now, go. I am sending you to Pharaoh to bring my people the Israelites out of Egypt.'" (Exodus 3:5-10)

"Do not come any closer…. Take off your sandals, for the place where you are standing is holy ground."

How do you react when God says that? Well, of course, you stop and take off your sandals! Can you imagine that moment when you realize that you are standing in the very presence of God? Knowing that God has declared the very ground you stand on holy must be an amazing feeling. Moses found himself in a divine moment, listening to an impossible dilemma, and about to receive a God-sized call.

Divine Moments

Although we don't realize it, we can all experience divine moments. I believe that God, from time to time, gives us a moment that is so entirely consumed by His presence that we know the very ground on which we stand is, for that moment, holy. I remember numerous times when the presence of God would just carry me away as I allowed myself to be lost in His presence. I have to tell you, there is nothing like it.

We need to pursue these moments, because it is then that we get a very clear understanding of God's divine presence. It's not that we could explain or somehow reproduce that presence; it is just that we learn to know Him. We learn to recognize Him. We learn to love Him. Unfortunately, instead of pursuing these moments, we often choose to run away from them. Fear, pride or ignorance gets in our way. Simply put, we should never let anything get in the way of a profound experience with God.

Impossible Dilemmas

There are so many things in our lives that seem impossible. The list of impossibilities is not limited to a single person or culture. The "impossibles" in life range from personal to global issues and the one thing they have in common is a seemingly insurmountable set of odds against resolution.

God almost always calls us to deal with the "impossibles" in our lives, because in God's sight, our "impossibles" are nothing more than miracles in the making. With God, everything is possible. The slavery of the Israelites and cruelty of the Egyptians that faced Moses was every bit as complex and impossible as any global political issue on the pages of today's newspapers. This was definitely an "impossible" problem, but God saw it and was ready to do something about it.

God's plan seemed even more improbable than the problem seemed impossible. Not only was God planning to free the Israelites from the most powerful nation on earth, He was planning to give them land for their nation that was already inhabited! There was Pharaoh and then there were fortified cities all standing between Israel and God's promise. This really was an impossible challenge. Perhaps Moses, for just a moment, felt sorry for the poor soul God called to do that job!

God-sized Call

I like steak. I don't order just any steak. I don't want a little pittance of meat that would have been better used as beginning ingredients for a decent hamburger. I don't want the kiddie portion. I want a man-sized steak. (I now have the attention of any hungry male reading along!) Well, just like I want a man-sized steak, God is looking for followers who are willing to accept a God-sized call.

Look, if the problem was simple enough for us to find and achieve the answer on our own, we would have no need for God. Instead, He calls us to deal with issues that are beyond our abilities. He sends us to places that are outside of our comfort zones. He presses us into service in areas where we feel inadequate and incapable. Why? He wants us to trust Him for solutions to the "impossibles" in our lives. He wants to work miracles through our faith in Him and our trust in His heart and abilities. He is a miracle-working God. He is looking for miracle-believing people.

So, when you think you have heard that call but you are not sure because you know it is beyond you, hold on. When you accept that call, you step out of the comfortable world of your own impossibilities and into the powerful world of God's miraculous possibilities!

Personal Thoughts:

TRUST THE LORD

"But Moses said to God, 'Who am I, that I should go to Pharaoh and bring the Israelites out of Egypt?' And God said, 'I will be with you. And this will be the sign to you that it is I who have sent you: When you have brought the people out of Egypt, you will worship God on this mountain.'" (Exodus 3:11-12)

It never fails. Every time I get on an airplane and we begin to take off, my prayer life improves. I really am not fond of flying. (I am, however, less fond of days upon days of driving.) When that plane starts to take off, I will put away any book or magazine I may be reading and sit quietly. While on the outside I look fine, inside I am begging with God: "Lord, I know You are in charge and I trust You with my life. I know that if today my life ends, I will find myself in Heaven with You. Please take care of Tina and the boys, and please don't let it hurt too much. Thanks, Amen!" I usually pray that prayer numerous times until the plane levels out and the ride becomes smooth.

The problem I have with flying is not a lack of trust in God. The problem I have is a lack of trust in the physical laws that allow a few tons of metal and a few hundred humans to be hurled through

171

the air in a tube for hundreds or thousands of miles. While I know that many people, much smarter than me, designed and built this plane, I still worry. I obviously have enough trust in them to get on the plane, but I do not have enough trust to be comfortable with the experience. Perhaps trust is one of the most difficult traits we are called to develop.

Moses was not overly confident in his own abilities. He quickly saw that he was not capable of the task God was calling him to do. He spends much of the next couple of chapters explaining to God what God already knows. Listen, you are not capable of accomplishing grcat things for God on your own. God knows all of your weaknesses and failures. Still, He chooses you for the task. Knowing all of your issues, He trusts you to do more than you are comfortable attempting. Why? Because He will help you.

Sometimes in our lives we are forced to enter God's will much like I do airplanes. Trusting enough to get on board, but not convinced that it is such a good idea. The only answer to this is time and experience. Time allows us to know our situation and understand our calling better. Experience helps us to know what to expect and to stop feeling so insecure. While time and experience do not help much with current fear, it is important to realize that our fears will ease with time and experience.

Notice God's promise to Moses:

I will be with you. And this will be the sign to you that it is I who have sent you: When you have brought the people out of Egypt, you will worship God on this mountain. (Exodus 3:12)

Did you notice that the confirmation of God's calling comes after the arrival of God's miracle? After the Israelites are freed from slavery, God brings them to this mountain to worship. Then Moses will know that he has accomplished the task God has given him. In other words, we have to find the faith to move forward in God's call before God's miracle becomes a reality in our lives.

So the question seems obvious: "How long before I am comfortable with this seemingly impossible thing God is calling me to do?" Well, I'm not sure. I've been flying for more than 16 years now; I'll let you know when my faith in the physics of flying matches my faith in the Father of life. For now, let your faith outweigh your fear and miracles are a distinct possibility in your future!

Personal Thoughts:

SPEAK THE WORD

"Moses said to the LORD, 'O Lord, I have never been eloquent, neither in the past nor since you have spoken to your servant. I am slow of speech and tongue.' The LORD said to him, 'Who gave man his mouth? Who makes him deaf or mute? Who gives him sight or makes him blind? Is it not I, the LORD? Now go; I will help you speak and will teach you what to say.'" (Exodus 4:10-12)

Let's be clear, we are often called to follow God into areas that are terribly uncomfortable for us. In Moses' case, the last thing he wanted to be called to do was speak in front of large crowds. He just wasn't very good at it, but that was exactly what God had called him to do. He was to speak the Word of God to Pharaoh, the Egyptians, the Israelites, and ultimately, to followers of God for thousands of years to come. Even today, we hear the voice of Moses as we read through the Old Testament.

Trust God's Plan

"The LORD said to him, 'Who gave man his mouth? Who makes him deaf or mute? Who gives him sight or makes him blind? Is it not I, the LORD? Now go'"

So why would God expect us to do something that makes us uncomfortable? Why would God call Moses to a life of public speaking when he was not a good speaker? Simply put, because God knew what Moses was capable of even if Moses was uncomfortable with the prospect. God is the one who made Moses. He designed Moses' mouth and mind. He prepared Moses to do the very things he was now being asked to do. Moses did not feel capable, but God knew he was.

In our own lives, we are often insecure about our abilities. We think God has called us to things that we are incapable of doing. In reality, that is just not going to happen. God knew what He wanted you to do before you were ever born. He designed you to accomplish His plan and equipped you with everything you would need. Whatever it is God has called you to, you can be certain that He has and will continue to equip you to succeed.

Trust God's Help

"I will help you speak and will teach you what to say."

I will never forget the question: "What would you attempt for God if failure was not possible?" That question changed my perspective. I used to ask myself: "What am I capable of accomplishing?" Now I ask: "What is God capable of accomplishing through me?" These are very different questions. The first one focuses on my own abilities and is limited by my own contacts, drive and talents. The second focuses on God's abilities and is limited only by my willingness to let God use me.

In reality, God wants to use all of us in miraculous ways. He could use us to speak truth to a person who will not listen to anyone else. He could use us to show love to a person who does not have anyone else. God can use us in an unlimited number of ways to help make lives better and to change the world. He never leaves us to work alone. He helps us in every difficulty and empowers us for every challenge.

Trust the Holy Spirit

"He said to them: 'It is not for you to know the times or dates the Father has set by his own authority. But you will receive power when the Holy Spirit comes on you; and you will be my witnesses in Jerusalem, and in all Judea and Samaria, and to the ends of the earth.'" (Acts 1:7-8)

In the book of Acts, we once again find God calling His followers to a task that is bigger than they could imagine. A church must be established and a world must be changed. All of this must be done by about 120 frightened and confused followers huddled in an upstairs room. God had a secret weapon. That day the promise of the Holy Spirit became a reality. That day the disciples came to understand the promise we have just read.

The Holy Spirit is in our lives to empower and embolden us. He can take the meekest of us and boldly speak the truth. He will give us the words to speak and the courage to speak them. He will help us to understand the situations we find ourselves in and help us to overcome the obstacles we face. The Holy Spirit will come alongside us, walk with us, talk with us, weep with us, stand with us, suffer with us, overcome with us, and speak with and for us.

God has not left us alone in this great work we are given. He has arranged it so that He can be with us every step of the way. Do not be afraid. Announce the call God has given you. Declare the truth God has revealed to you. Accept the challenge God has designed for you. Praise the God who lives in you and works through you!

So, what would you attempt for God if failure was not possible?

Personal Thoughts:

UNLEASH THE VISION

"Moses and Aaron brought together all the elders of the Israelites, and Aaron told them everything the LORD had said to Moses. He also performed the signs before the people, and they believed. And when they heard that the LORD was concerned about them and had seen their misery, they bowed down and worshiped." (Exodus 4:29-31)

There comes a point with every God-given vision when we must call together a group of people and tell them our goals. This is truly a frightening moment. "What if they don't believe in me?" "What if they laugh at the very thought?" "What if I am wrong?" Terror can spin through your mind at an alarming rate. In some cases, you would just as soon miss the blessing as face the potential of rejection. A public statement of a personal calling requires proper planning, provision and praise.

Proper Planning

"Moses and Aaron brought together all the elders of the Israelites, and Aaron told them everything the LORD had said to Moses."

One mistake that many well-meaning and truly called believers make is not taking the time to plan out the work God has given. Now some of you would like to ask: "But shouldn't we just move forward and let God worry about the plan? Isn't that what faith is all about?" The answer is no. Moving forward without proper planning is not faith; it is at the least, presumption, and at the worst, laziness.

God gave each of us a wonderful mind that has the capacity to plan and organize. He certainly meant for us to use that mind as we work on the calling He has placed on our lives. God gives us our marching orders and then allows us the privilege of planning out the route. While it is true that He will adjust our course from time to time and tweak our plan, it also is true that He expects us to think through how we plan to accomplish the task He has given us.

Proper Provision

"He also performed the signs before the people, and they believed."

Here is the difficult intersection of faith and reason. There is a careful balance between what we know we have and what we believe, in faith, God will provide. We should always be careful to watch for the fine line between faith and presumption.

To simply move forward without proper planning is to presume on the goodness of God. Far too often, we simply expect God to come through because we want Him to and we don't consider His call or His will. This places our desires above God's desires and is entirely inappropriate. The issue is God's plan, not our preferences. We should never presume on the goodness of God.

On the other hand, to avoid moving forward in what we know God has called us to do simply because we do not have every dollar or every answer, is a lack of faith. Wherever God calls, God provides. His provision may not come before we reach our deadline for commitment. When we are forced to commit to what we know to be His plan before we see full provision for that plan, we step out in faith.

Balancing these two realities is one of the most difficult lessons to learn in our Christian walk. It is rarely completely clear what we are to do and it is rare that all the resources are on hand at the start of our work. Faith is required and yet presumption is dangerous. We must be careful to recognize and listen to the voice of God at every step of the way on our journey. Just like the powerful miracles God performed for Moses, our work can be punctuated by the miraculous entrance of the powerful hand of God.

Proper Praise

"And when they heard that the LORD was concerned about them and had seen their misery, they bowed down and worshiped."

When God's people receive God's plan and expect God's power to bring God's deliverance, God's people should praise Him! One of the distinguishing aspects of a life lived in the will of God is that all the glory for any success goes to God alone. The true servant of God will not take any glory due to God for himself.

After seeing the powerful miracles that God was empowering Moses to perform, no one misunderstood the source of the power. No one said, "Wow! Moses is incredible!" Instead they were impressed with the presence of God in the life of Moses. They were moved by God's attention to their misery and excited by His presence in their midst.

When people see and recognize God's leading in our visionary plans and God's provision along the way, they will stop and give Him praise and know He is present in their situation and concerned for their future. Remember, when God gives you a vision, don't keep it a secret; UNLEASH IT!

Personal Notes:

LIGHTEN THE LOAD

"The next day Moses took his seat to serve as judge for the people, and they stood around him from morning till evening. When his father-in-law saw all that Moses was doing for the people, he said, 'What is this you are doing for the people? Why do you alone sit as judge, while all these people stand around you from morning till evening?' Moses answered him, 'Because the people come to me to seek God's will. Whenever they have a dispute, it is brought to me, and I decide between the parties and inform them of God's decrees and laws.' Moses' father-in-law replied, 'What you are doing is not good. You and these people who come to you will only wear yourselves out. The work is too heavy for you; you cannot handle it alone.'" (Exodus 18:13-18)

Any vision that is truly from God will be more than we can handle alone. Simply put, if you are capable of accomplishing what you set out to do, why would you need God? In fact, God is just not going to give you a "you-sized" vision. He will give you a "God-sized" vision. Then He will look for you to lean on Him and His people to accomplish the goal. To really accomplish a "God-sized" goal, we will need to change the way we manage our lives and our work. "God-sized" goals require multiplied effort. Moses' father-in-law, Jethro, understood that, and advised Moses to begin multiplying himself so that he would not need to continue exhausting himself.

Powerful not Personal

Nothing significant has ever been accomplished by one person alone. Significance always requires teamwork. In fact, the larger the team the more significant the potential outcome can be. Large groups of people working toward one single goal are not even considered teams or accomplishments; they are called movements. In a movement, an entire culture can be involved and historic changes can be made. Movements truly change history.

The problem is that most of us are more interested in personal acclaim than we are in powerful results. We would rather have people see us as smart, brave or strong, and we hesitate to give credit to others who work with us or support us. With this type of self-centered attitude, we cannot expect to accomplish great things. In fact, we really should not expect to accomplish anything of lasting value.

As Moses' father-in-law looked at the crowds gathered around seeking answers to their problems, he must have wondered: "Do these people think Moses is the only one with ideas or answers? This is just not a good idea." No matter how important the attention made Moses feel, the work was not being accomplished. If things did not change, and soon, this movement would fall apart, and so would Moses. Moses had to become less important, personally, to become more significant, historically.

Effective not Impressive

So, let me ask you a question. Would you rather impress people around you or accomplish the goal set before you? Honestly, both may not be possible. Often in leadership, you will be forced to choose between personally impressing those around you and reaching the goal.

Moses was faced with this moment when Jethro pointed out the inefficiency of the process. Moses would never get through all of the needs of everyone by himself. He would have to empower other people to do the work that He was currently doing. While less responsibility may seem to be a good thing, it also means the loss of personal praise and power. Until now, Moses would hear things like, "I just don't know how we would do it without you!" "You are so smart!" "God certainly uses you!" "Thank God for you, Moses!"

Moses was now going to need to empower someone else to be smart and insightful. He was going to have to allow someone else to have all the answers and be used by God. In the end, all that praise would go to someone else. Praise and popularity like that can be a tough thing to let go, but effectively accomplishing the goal must be more important.

Inclusive not Exclusive

"There is no limit to what can be accomplished if you do not care who gets the credit." I am not certain who said that first, but I first heard it from John Maxwell. Maxwell is one of the most respected teachers on leadership in the country. For years, he has taught leaders to share the load and the credit with those who follow them. This concept is not new to Maxwell; he read it in Exodus.

Jethro actually became the very first leadership guru. He looked at an impossible situation and broke it down into a simple and effective plan to get the job done and train leaders to lead. The truth is that if you never let anyone help you, you never teach anyone to replace you. That means when you are gone, the movement is over.

Jethro knew that teaching people to lead groups of 10, 50, 100 or even 1,000 would develop leaders who could carry the load after he was gone and after Moses was gone. They would, in fact, create a plan that would develop leaders for generations to come. Including others in leading the vision that God has given you is the very best way to ensure that your work will not only outgrow you, but it will outlive you.

Personal Thoughts:

JOIN THE TEAM

"So Joshua fought the Amalekites as Moses had ordered, and Moses, Aaron and Hur went to the top of the hill. As long as Moses held up his hands, the Israelites were winning, but whenever he lowered his hands, the Amalekites were winning. When Moses' hands grew tired, they took a stone and put it under him and he sat on it. Aaron and Hur held his hands up – one on one side, one on the other – so that his hands remained steady till sunset. So Joshua overcame the Amalekite army with the sword." (Exodus 17:10-13)

We all know Moses and most of us know Joshua. Fewer know Aaron. Does anyone know Hur? It would seem, based on popularity alone, that Hur was a minor part of this moment in history. I mean, if we don't remember his name, how important is he?

The history of the Israelites would be dramatically different if he had not been there. On this day, in this battle, Hur, a man we don't remember, was just as important as anyone else present. The help he gave to Moses literally brought victory to the nation. You may think that his contribution was small or insignificant, but in reality, God used Hur in a mighty way.

Often people don't get involved in ministry because they think they have too little to offer. Nothing could be further from the truth. In reality, everyone has a significant role to play in building the church. God has specific and important roles for each of us in His ultimate plan for mankind. We should never underestimate the importance of what God has for us to do. While it may be true that God uses some in very public and highly visible ways and others in more quiet and unseen ways, this is simply a matter of visibility, not importance.

I often will ask people who they think the most important person is at a Wal-Mart store. The answers will range from the CEO to the stockers. The true answer comes down to two individuals, the greeter and the cashier. You will form your opinion of that store based on your experience with one of those two people. Wal-Mart can have the best CEO in the business, but if the greeters and cashiers at individual stores are not kind or efficient, the company will suffer loss.

The church works in much the same way. While we talk about musicians, preachers or teachers, we are most impacted by greeters or children's workers. People can find good music or a good speaker in any number of settings. They can find concerts, speeches, music festivals, political events and many other forms of entertainment to fill those needs. What people are looking for is a Christ-centered ministry that really cares about them, their needs, and their family. They want to be greeted by someone who really cares that they are there, and they want to be treated like family.

So, let's assume that your strongest gift is being nice to people. Guess what, you just became one of the most important workers in the church. You could be the very face of God's love to someone who has come with a need. If your strongest gift is taking care of children, you are one of the most important workers in the church. People need to know that their children are being taught and cared for in a loving and safe environment. They cannot hear the message of peace while worrying about the safety of their children.

You may enjoy landscaping and cleaning so that people see a love and care for the house of God. Counseling can provide people with a Christian perspective to life's problems. Support groups see to it that people do not go through life's toughest times and struggles alone. Food ministries exist so that people find hospitality in the house of

God. Youth ministries help teens go through some of life's most difficult decisions with the help and support of loving adults and caring peers. The list of ministries could literally go on.

The truth of the matter is that you are skilled for ministry, and the ministry you are skilled for is important. The question then is not if you have anything to offer. The question is when will you get started?

Let me suggest NOW!

Personal Thoughts:

6

TRUST

Becoming a person of Integrity

REMAIN TRUTHFUL

"Again, you have heard that it was said to the people long ago, 'Do not break your oath, but keep the oaths you have made to the Lord.' But I tell you, Do not swear at all: either by heaven, for it is God's throne; or by the earth, for it is his footstool; or by Jerusalem, for it is the city of the Great King. And do not swear by your head, for you cannot make even one hair white or black. Simply let your 'Yes' be 'Yes,' and your 'No,' 'No'; anything beyond this comes from the evil one." (Matthew 5:33-37)

"I swear to tell the truth, the whole truth, and nothing but the truth." Now there is a pledge to live by. Hearing that pledge most often causes us to think of someone about to testify in court. However, should that not be true of a Christian at all times? Shouldn't a Christian be known as someone who always tells the truth, the whole truth, and nothing but the truth? The answer is yes.

Jesus encountered a society that did not take truth very seriously. During the New Testament period, it was common to swear by almost anything except the most holy name of God, Yaweh. Many of these oaths were not taken seriously and no one fully expected them to be fulfilled. Therefore, there was a culture of lies rather than a culture of truth. Jesus, as is so often His way, confronted the situation head-on.

"Again, you have heard that it was said to the people long ago, 'Do not break your oath, but keep the oaths you have made to the Lord.' But I tell you, Do not swear at all"

Once again, Jesus looks directly into the culture of his day and calls for change. The simple call of our Savior to all those who would follow Him is to be honest. I always get the question: "OK, fine. I'm supposed to tell the truth, but what if telling the truth would hurt someone?" The reality is that not telling someone a painful truth only makes the pain worse when the truth is finally revealed. If the dress is ugly in the store, it will not get any better by the time the party starts! We need to be honest, even painfully honest, with everyone in our lives. This is not a matter of being rude. Honesty does not have to be brutal. It simply means being honest. I would rather work with someone who would tell me the truth about their feelings, even the negative ones, than someone who would try to make me feel good even when I am wrong.

Jesus calls us to let our "Yes be Yes" and our "No, No." In other words, quit trying to use clever words to hide true meanings. Just tell the simple and plain truth. There really is nothing complex about this thought. If it is true, share it. If it is not, don't. Do you realize how revolutionary that would be in many work and home environments? No more reading between the lines. No more guessing at what was really meant. No more mistrust of coworkers or family members. Wouldn't that be great?!

Unfortunately, not everyone is going to follow Jesus' teaching on this point, but we should. The world should look at us and see people of truth. They should never have to question whether a Christian has lied to them. They should look to us as the most trustworthy group of people in the entire society. Integrity demands that we be honest. God demands that we live lives of integrity.

So, perhaps you remember the old game Truth or Dare? I have a new one for you. I dare you to tell the truth. Stop telling the little lies that seem to make your life easier. Leave behind the half-truths that hide just enough so that no one is suspicious. Change your attitude toward the truth and just let yes mean yes and no mean no.

Personal Thoughts:

REMAIN TRANSPARENT

"When I came to you, brothers, I did not come with eloquence or superior wisdom as I proclaimed to you the testimony about God. For I resolved to know nothing while I was with you except Jesus Christ and him crucified. I came to you in weakness and fear, and with much trembling. My message and my preaching were not with wise and persuasive words, but with a demonstration of the Spirit's power, so that your faith might not rest on men's wisdom, but on God's power." (1 Corinthians 2:1-5)

People tend not to like politicians. That's kind of sad if you think about it. We tend not to like the very people we entrust with the power to run our country. A little scary if you ask me. So why do people tend not to like politicians? I think the answer is a matter of transparency. We are not looking for someone who is perfect or someone who is brilliant. We are looking for someone who is real. Someone you can look at and see who they really are. We have seen plenty of fakes and phonies that we long for the real thing. We are looking for integrity, but integrity requires honesty. Honesty requires transparency. Unfortunately, we are terribly lacking in these characteristics among politicians.

Transparency is a willingness to let others see you for who you really are. It is a willingness to share the deepest parts of your being and your nature with others. Transparency is risky business. When you let others get to know you on that deep level, there is the possibility that they will not like what they see. They may even use some of the less flattering things they find against you. Transparency can be a painful business. However, it is all part of a lifestyle of honesty.

When Paul came to the Corinthians, he was capable of debating with the very best that his opponents had to offer. He was intelligent, well educated and passionate, yet he did not approach them in that manner. Why? At Corinth, Paul encountered plenty of people who wanted to debate his philosophy and teachings. In this large city, there were as many as 12 temples to different gods. This fact coupled with the Greek love for debate would serve as a strong temptation to enter into the loud discussions of the day, but Paul refused.

Truth be known, very few people are won to the faith through debate. Most are won through lives of obvious and real faith. Paul simply made a decision. I am not going to debate you; I am going to let my life show and let my integrity debate for me. He would *"know nothing … except Jesus Christ and him crucified."* There would be no attempt to prove his intellect, only an attempt to display his character. In this setting, Paul would serve as a positive example for a group of Christians who desperately needed one.

In my experience, it seems that people who are the most educated and intellectual among us are usually not looking for someone to debate. They are not looking for someone to mentally spar. Not when it comes to faith or spiritual matters. They are looking for the same thing everyone else wants. They want a real faith that can change lives. They seek an authentic truth that is clearly displayed in the hearts and lives of those who claim to know it. They want something real.

In our lives, we need to be certain that we really are who and what we say we are. We preach sermons every day to the power of God for changing lives. We speak through our actions and our attitudes to the reality of the Gospel we say we believe. We are walking billboards for Christianity. As such, we better be real. We must truly become like Christ and stop just acting like Christians. Our faith must be the driving force in all of our decisions and plans, even when it is not convenient, comfortable or profitable.

Simply put, if we were to become so transparent that everyone could see into our hearts, what would they find there? Would they find a true believer or a politician?

Personal Thoughts:

REMAIN TEACHABLE

"Moses said to the LORD, 'You have been telling me, Lead these people, but you have not let me know whom you will send with me. You have said, I know you by name and you have found favor with me. If you are pleased with me, teach me your ways so I may know you and continue to find favor with you. Remember that this nation is your people.'" (Exodus 33:12-13)

I don't know if you have noticed this yet or not, but stuff changes. I mean everything changes sooner or later. Methods and techniques that once worked have now become obsolete. In the Internet and World Wide Web age, things can change at light speed. You walk out of the door of a computer store with the latest technology and then find that it is obsolete by the time you get home! Changes come fast in today's world.

In a changing environment, one of the most important traits to learn is teachability. Now, my spell check says that is not a real word, but it is a real state of mind. It is a state of mind that understands that there is always much more to learn. It is a state of mind that comprehends that there are many ways to solve a given problem. It is a state of mind that understands there is no point, in this life, where we have learned all that we need to know. We will never reach a point of expertise that does not require change.

Moses was obviously one of the best followers of God in history. I don't read any other account of God being as close to a human being as He was to Moses. Yet here, late in his life, we find Moses making a request of God: *"If you are pleased with me, teach me your ways so I may know you and continue to find favor with you."* During a personal encounter with God, Moses asks for a lesson in living and making God happy. Moses understood.

Learning is a life-long process. There is never a time when there are no lessons left to be learned. There is always someone or some situation that can help us to better understand our world. God always has new situations for us to conquer and new lessons for us to learn. He is constantly building into our lives the experiences and understanding that will make us better servants of Him. More than He wants us to be intelligent, God wants us to be teachable. More than He wants us to have ability, God wants us to have teachability.

Moses' request pleased God. It is in this passage that Moses asks God to always stay with him and the Israelites. That request, too, pleased God. Moses seemed to understand what God wanted from him at every turn. Although Moses made his share of mistakes, he was always willing to own up to them and move past them. He was willing to learn from God's wisdom and from his own stupidity. Moses knew, in no uncertain terms, that God was Almighty and that he was not. And that pleased God. *"Then Moses said, 'Now show me your glory'" (Exodus 33:18)*, and God did.

To see the glory of God in our lives, we must constantly be willing to learn from the will, the mind and the Spirit of God. We must remain flexible as God uses us and trains us. We must remain teachable as God leads us and instructs us. We must remain available as God calls us and sends us. In the end, we will see God's glory in our lives to the same degree that we surrender to His authority in our lives. More surrender = more glory. More flexibility and teachability = more surrender.

So, stuff changes. And that ain't all bad.

Personal Notes:

REMAIN WISE

"The proverbs of Solomon son of David, king of Israel: for attaining wisdom and discipline; for understanding words of insight; for acquiring a disciplined and prudent life, doing what is right and just and fair; for giving prudence to the simple, knowledge and discretion to the young – let the wise listen and add to their learning, and let the discerning get guidance – for understanding proverbs and parables, the sayings and riddles of the wise. The fear of the LORD is the beginning of knowledge, but fools despise wisdom and discipline." (Proverbs 1:1-7)

Wisdom is not knowledge. For something known and not applied is merely trivia. Wisdom is knowledge applied, facts put to use, information put to work. Wisdom is not knowledge; it is more.

I have known people in my life who were very good at memorizing information in order to pass a test or achieve a diploma. Over time, they amass a great deal of knowledge or information. The problem is they don't know how the information they possess goes together. They have no concept of how it could be useful or practical. It seems to them that practicality is not the point. Just knowing is the point. Information is the goal. But it isn't.

I have known others who insisted on understanding how all the information they were amassing fit together. For them the question was never, "What must I memorize to pass the test?" The question was always, "What must I learn to understand why and how this works?" They wanted the information they were gathering to improve their lives and the lives of others around them. Understanding is the goal. And wisdom is the result.

Gaining wisdom is not an easy process. It does not come with the passing of a test or the earning of a degree. There is no formula that can be memorized and recited. Wisdom is what makes us more than the animals and machines in which we share the planet. Wisdom is understanding and reason. Gaining wisdom requires a great deal of thought. Wisdom requires a great deal of experience. Wisdom often requires a great deal of pain.

A Thinking Believer

All too often Christians seem to just turn off their brains and go into some type of auto-pilot lifestyle. We just choose to believe because we choose to believe. We don't want anyone to challenge our faith or ask difficult questions about our beliefs. We somehow have equated walking in ignorance with walking in faith. The two are by no means the same thing.

Our faith is as intellectual as it is inspirational. God has given us a faith that challenges us at every level. He has given us a world view that can help make sense of the world around us. God has blessed us with a faith that stands up to the most rigorous debates and the most difficult questions. If you are following without thinking, you are missing the better part of the peace and grace that God has intended for you to have. God's truth makes sense and brings understanding.

An Experienced Believer

Modern society has devalued old age. That is a sad loss to modern society. I will never forget stepping onto the pulpit for the first time in Kings Mountain, North Carolina. Mr. Natan Kelly was there on the second row looking me over. Mr. Kelly had been a believer about twice as long as I had been alive. The church had many members who had been led to faith by Mr. Kelly and everyone knew that he was truly a man of God. Needless to say, I was a bit intimidated.

Mr. Kelly's faith had stood through many years, many trials, and many young preachers. He listened, he said amen, and he encouraged me. Over the next few years, I learned to listen to Mr. Kelly, Margie Bridges and Miss Sarah because I could learn from their experiences. I did not always find things that were useful in my generation, but I did find truth that was timeless. When it comes to wisdom, there is no replacement for experience.

A Scarred Believer

Perhaps the greatest teacher of all is pain. We learn quickly and the lessons seem to stick when they come coupled with pain. The questions surrounding painful experiences are profound. They are not the type of insights that can be learned in a classroom setting by young students who do not know personal pain. No, these are the lessons that scar us. These are the stories that we tell because people ask about the obvious and visible signs of our pain.

This painful wisdom is perhaps the most important of all. It comes from the depths of our experience and is helpful to those who find themselves at their end. For them, debate is not helpful. Information is not comforting. Hope is required. To look at the scars of someone who has been there and see healing is the greatest encouragement possible. To know that someone else understands and cares, gives strength and hope to an otherwise dark future. Wisdom bought with scars holds great value.

So take time to think. Take time to consider what God is teaching you. Take time to turn some of that knowledge into wisdom and let God use your wisdom in ways that are profound and eternal. Let your life be driven by a wise purpose and not just a trivial pursuit.

Personal Notes:

REMAIN TRUE

*"Finally, be strong in the Lord and in his mighty power.
Put on the full armor of God so that you can take your
stand against the devil's schemes. For our struggle is not
against flesh and blood, but against the rulers, against the
authorities, against the powers of this dark world and
against the spiritual forces of evil in the heavenly realms.
Therefore put on the full armor of God, so that when the day
of evil comes, you may be able to stand your ground, and
after you have done everything, to stand. Stand firm then,
with the belt of truth buckled around your waist, with the
breastplate of righteousness in place, and with your feet fitted
with the readiness that comes from the gospel of peace. In
addition to all this, take up the shield of faith, with which
you can extinguish all the flaming arrows of the evil one.
Take the helmet of salvation and the sword of the Spirit,
which is the word of God. And pray in the Spirit on all
occasions with all kinds of prayers and requests. With this
in mind, be alert and always keep on praying for all the
saints." (Ephesians 6:10-18)*

So, do you want to have a significant
IMPACT for Christ? Then be forewarned. It is
not going to be easy. There will be depressing and
difficult days. There will be enemies who come
against you. In the difficulties of this journey, we

must work at taking a firm stand on what we believe. We must do everything to stand in the righteousness God has called us to, and even then, we must stand firm.

Far too many well-meaning believers simply fail to hold on for the long haul. They do good and even accomplish great things for a time, and then they fall by the side of the road and fail to carry through on the promise of their work and their word. The world sees this and begins to call our faith weak and even fake. But we cannot allow our work to end like this. We must remain true to what God has called us to do. We must remain strong and resolute as we take this journey. Holiness and faithfulness do not come easy, but they are always worth the price.

Remaining true for the long haul will require some tools. Truthfulness, righteousness, readiness, faith, salvation, the Word, and prayer are all absolutely essential. Without these tools we cannot expect to be successful in our quest for holy living. To remain true, we must lean on these weapons and on others who travel with us.

Remember as you march forward towards God's best for you, He has given you the weapons necessary to win. He has not left you alone. God

Himself is on the journey with us. His presence and His power will sustain us in difficult days. His calling and His purpose will animate our lives and guide our steps. His love will strengthen our hearts and His sacrifice will steel our will. God will never leave us or forsake us. He will travel with us and protect us.

One of the things that I have always wanted to avoid in my life is being nothing more than a flash in the pan. I don't want to leave a firecracker legacy. One that bursts onto the scene with a great deal of noise and a little bit of heat, but just as quickly vanishes and is never heard from again. I would rather start a wildfire of love and devotion for my Lord. Unlike a firecracker, a wildfire often starts slowly and quietly in an unseen location. It burns quietly in some remote location for a long time before finally catching the attention of the firefighters. By the time those who would douse the flames arrive, there is movement. Hot, scorching, determined movement.

It takes a great deal of time and effort to stop a wildfire. And so it can be with the Gospel. It can burn hot and determined into the cultures and lives of every person on the planet. It can overtake vast areas regardless of local government or philosophy.

The Gospel can burn through the perceived walls mankind has erected between cultures and races and ideologies. If allowed to burn, it can burn away the old dead ideas of the past and make room for the beautiful, lush gardens of the future.

But this burning movement requires a starting place. More correctly, it requires a starting person. It will require someone willing to burn hot for the Lord in obscurity for a long while. Someone must withstand the heat, the time, and the difficulty of starting a movement. Someone must pay the price. Honestly, that is who I want to be. Not a builder of a church, but a builder of a movement. Not a successful pastor, but a surrendered servant. Not a solitary saint, but a sold-out leader. In this way, we build a movement that really changes the world around us. In this way, we build something that out-lives us. That kind of **IMPACT** is my goal.

What about you?

Personal Thoughts:

ABOUT THE AUTHOR

Mike Hilson is the Senior Pastor of the New Life Wesleyan Church in La Plata, Maryland. Starting out in 1999 with a congregation of less than 100 attendees, New Life Church has tremendously grown and multiplied into several churches and venues with now more than 4,000 in regular attendance. In addition, New Life Church has a significant presence in local and international relief work. Along with his work as senior pastor, Mike currently serves as the Assistant District Superintendent of the Chesapeake District as well as serving on the Board of Trustees at Southern Wesleyan University. He lives in La Plata with his wife, Tina, who is the Director of Grow Ministries for New Life Church. They have three sons, Robert, Stephen and Joshua, who have taken this journey of ministry with them.

Made in the USA
Columbia, SC
05 December 2021